Corrado Tommasi-Crudeli, Charles Cramond Dick

The Climate of Rome and the Roman Malaria

Corrado Tommasi-Crudeli, Charles Cramond Dick

The Climate of Rome and the Roman Malaria

ISBN/EAN: 9783744781442

Printed in Europe, USA, Canada, Australia, Japan

Cover: Foto ©ninafisch / pixelio.de

More available books at **www.hansebooks.com**

THE CLIMATE OF ROME

AND THE

ROMAN MALARIA

BY

PROFESSOR TOMMASI-CRUDELI

TRANSLATED FROM THE ITALIAN

BY

CHARLES CRAMOND DICK

LONDON
J. & A. CHURCHILL
11, NEW BURLINGTON STREET

1892

PREFACE.

In the year 1885, Professor Corrado Tommasi-Crudeli delivered a course of lectures at the inauguration of the Institute of Hygiene, attached to the University of Rome. These were afterwards collected and published by him under the title of "Il Clima di Roma."

The present, is a translation of that work, which has been revised and corrected up to date, by Professor Tommasi-Crudeli himself.

To my friend, Dr. Eager of Northwoods, near Bristol, I am indebted for the proper rendering of the medical terms. I am likewise indebted to Dr. Blanc of Cannes, and other kind friends, for many valuable corrections and suggestions.

THE TRANSLATOR.

September, 1892.

TABLE OF CONTENTS.

CHAPTER I.
The Climate of Rome in its General Outlines — PAGE 1

CHAPTER II.
The Roman Soil — 16

CHAPTER III.
The Waters of the Roman Region — 30

CHAPTER IV.
The Roman Malaria — 53

CHAPTER V.
The Autochthonous Production of Malaria in the Territory of Rome and of the Agro; and the Sanitary Measures Proposed for Impeding its Development — 75

CHAPTER VI.
Forests in Connection with the Roman Malaria — 100

CHAPTER VII.
The Permanent Sanitation of the Agro Romano — 119

CHAPTER VIII.
The Preservation of Human Life in Malarious Countries — 135

THE CLIMATE OF ROME AND THE ROMAN MALARIA.

CHAPTER I.

THE CLIMATE OF ROME IN ITS GENERAL OUTLINES.

IN all questions relating to the climate of any particular locality many prejudices have to be overcome, and many preconceived ideas to be combated, before a correct notion can be formed of the subject itself, and a just appreciation of the conclusions arrived at. In dealing with the climate of Rome this is especially the case, for such erroneous notions have become fixed in the minds of most people, as to render the task of extirpating them almost hopeless. Ignorance, prejudice, conceit, infatuation, and personal interest, form a mighty array against which to do battle. Moreover, the difficulties of a just appreciation of the true state of things, have been enormously increased since Rome has been proclaimed the capital of Italy, because the most conflicting interests have been called into play. To listen to some, Rome is a pestiferous city, totally unsuited to be the capital of a modern state; according to others there is no city in Italy so healthy.

Some aver that the Campagna of Rome must always remain in its present condition, as it is quite incapable of any agricultural or hygienic improvement; whereas others assert that it can be rapidly converted into an Eden of delights, provided the particular method of sanitation advocated by each one, be adopted. During many years those exaggerations on either side—all of them equally unjustifiable—have agitated public opinion and excited acrimonious controversies;—have given rise to every kind of financial speculation, and sometimes have led astray the Italian Government, which since 1870 has assumed the sanitation of the Roman Campagna. It behoves us to form an impartial judgment of the Roman climate, amidst the chaos of disjointed and contradictory opinions, before estimating the value of the sanitary works which are about to be carried on in that region.

In the first place it would be well to come to a clear understanding as to the meaning of the word "climate," for in the ordinary acceptation of the term its sense is extremely limited. When the climate of a particular locality is spoken of, it is generally supposed to refer only to the meteorological facts of the place; that is to say, the usual physical condition of its atmosphere. Under such circumstances our task would be quickly accomplished. It would suffice to say that Rome has a maritime and temperate climate, inasmuch as it is only 20 kilometres distant in a straight line from the sea; and according to the observations made at the Collegio Romano its annual average temperature may be stated at $+ 16°$ C. We might also add that the average quantity of rain which falls there during the year is about 800 millimetres, that the average atmospheric pressure is calculated to be $762^{mm.}$, and the relative humidity of the same is 66° C.; and then wind up with a detailed account of the north, south, east, and west winds. But neither such, nor other meteorological details, into which I might enter, would be of any use for conveying the least idea of the real climate of

Rome. A climate consists entirely of other elements, and to form an adequate idea of it, it is necessary to study the many and various influences which its surrounding nature exercises upon human life.

The natural history of the world teaches us that the three indispensable elements of life are earth, air, and water; and the natural history of man shows that those elements, either directly or indirectly, are the factors of human life. By their combined action upon the life of man and of human societies, they constitute the climate in which we exist. Every modification of those elements, which may have a direct or indirect influence on human life, produces either beneficial or detrimental variations of climate—variations, that is to say, of the aggregate of those natural facts in which, and through which, human life exists.

Some of the modifications of the three great climatical elements are the result of natural events entirely independent of the existence of human societies in a given locality, whereas others are caused by the existence of man and of domestic animals in the locality. The *natural climate* of a place is determined by the former, and to the latter are due the numberless varieties of *acquired climates*, which are permanent or temporary, according as the modifying agencies of the natural climate of the place are permanent, or have been accidentally and temporarily introduced from without. The study of these acquired climates does not have any special interest in Rome. It may even be said that such a study offers a great deal less interest in Rome than in any other great city, inasmuch as the modifications made in the natural climate of Rome by the vicissitudes of human society there, are very limited.

The relative rarity of epidemics caused by direct contagion, such as small-pox, scarlatina, measles, and diphtheria, is conclusively proved by statistics. Moreover, the deterioration of the soil, of the air, and of the waters of Rome, by means of animal detritus and the morbific germs which it may contain, is not as great as might appear at first sight.

As a matter of fact, the new quarters of the city occupy ground, which, till 1870, had been used as vineyards and meadows for centuries : they had not been impregnated with human and animal excrement during those centuries, to any appreciable extent. Those grounds are now covered by buildings destined for the habitation of persons who lead a civilized existence, and constructed according to the most approved methods of drainage actually in use. If, besides, we consider that the greater portion of those new quarters is situated on the urban hills, so that the drains of the houses and of the streets can receive a sufficient fall ; and that drinking water is to be had in such abundance as to admit of the sewers being continually flushed by their overflow, even during the dry weather; we can readily understand that there is but slight danger of any poisonous infiltration in the subsoil of the new districts, provided that the public and private drains are properly looked to and kept in order.

But a danger exists where the drains of the new districts flow into the old sewers of the lower parts of the town, which do not allow a rapid discharge of the human detritus into the Tiber. In that case, the gases developed in the old sewers occasionally acquire a great tension ; and accumulate, owing to their small specific gravity, in the drains of the higher districts. Hence the offensive smells which are to be met with in some places, inasmuch as the tension of the sewer gases easily overcomes the atmospheric pressure, and allows them to disperse abroad and contaminate the air of the streets and houses.

In order to obviate this nuisance I have suggested the

fixing of ventilating pipes in the higher parts of the new sewers to carry off the greater portion of the noxious gases into a stratum of the atmosphere above the roofs of the highest houses. Should such a suggestion be adopted, and should, moreover, the works proposed by the engineer Vescovali be carried out, for separating the internal air of the sewers from the air of the streets and houses, the atmosphere of the new districts will be preserved from that mixture of gases which are injurious of themselves, and are rendered still more so, by the morbific germs which they hold in suspension. These gases cannot possibly emanate from the interstices of the subsoil, inasmuch as in the past this was never subject to the infiltration of organic detritus; nor is it at the present time, as the walls of the new sewers are impermeable. They can only proceed from the interior of the drains, and it is an easy matter, therefore, to prevent their mixing with the atmosphere of the streets and houses.

Nor is there any difficulty to be apprehended in preventing those gases from contaminating the drinking water of the new districts, most of which are supplied by the *Acqua Marcia*, which is carried in impermeable pipes into the reservoirs on the roofs of the houses. It must be admitted, however, that in every case where the overflow pipe communicates directly with the sewer, the gas from the latter ascends up the pipe and reaches the reservoirs, contaminating the water which they hold, with all the deleterious elements which it conveys. But it is very easy to cut off all direct communication between the overflow pipe and the sewer, thereby quickly removing all inconvenience and danger.

In the ancient parts of the city matters are on a different footing. The development of Rome in mediæval and papal times was principally in the plains of the ancient city; first of all, along the valley of the Tiber, and afterwards in the little valleys which separated and still continue partly to separate the Capitoline Hill from the Palatine, the Pincian from the Quirinal, the Quirinal from the Capitoline, the Capitoline from the Esquiline, and the Esquiline from the Cœlian. In ancient Rome, the inhabited districts were principally on the hills, and the greater portion of the dividing plains was occupied by the Campus Martius, the camp of Agrippa, the Villa Publica, the circuses, the theatres, and the amphitheatres; by some of the baths, and the Forums. The reason of this great divergence is this,—that after the depredations of the barbarians and the destruction of the aqueducts, the population collected together in those places where drinking water was easily found, either by drawing it from the Tiber, or from wells sunk to a short depth in the soil. At first sight it seems surprising that the water of the Tiber, which is always muddy, could have been the inducement to the population to settle on the banks of that river in order to obtain drinking water. But a miserable people, such as the Romans were at that time, who are in want of water and have not the means of obtaining a supply of a good quality from a distance, do not weigh matters very carefully, and make use of what comes to hand. Moreover, amongst the many strange notions on the subject of hygiene, which occasionally possess the minds of people, one of the most persistent was, that the waters of the Tiber contained some specific sanitary virtues. And so true is this, that in 1533, in the midst of the splendours of the Renaissance in art and literature, Pope Clement VII., when he went to France for the marriage of his niece Catherine de Medici, took with him, on the advice of Corti his doctor, a sufficient supply of Tiber water to last him during his absence.

Besides, the facility of obtaining drinking water from wells was much greater in the plains, where, by digging, it was often found at a much shorter distance from the surface than on the hills. If we look at the plan made by Vescovali of the water-bearing zone of Rome between the Gate of San Lorenzo and the Janiculum, passing along the Pantheon; we see how great a distance there is between the water-bearing zone and the surface of the soil on the Esquiline, the Viminal, and a great portion of the Quirinal. Nor could the extension of the city on those hills be, to any degree, assisted by conveying the *Acqua Vergine* thither, inasmuch as it has a very low pressure, and can only be distributed along the low-lying districts. It was for this reason that Sixtus V., when he wished to encourage the re-populating of those hills, bethought himself, as a preliminary measure, to convey to those heights a supply of drinking water. But in this he only partially succeeded, for the ancient *Acqua Alexandrina* (now the *Acqua Felice*) which he brought into Rome from the Agro Colonnese, was not sufficient, either in quantity or quality, to meet the requirements of the numerous population of those districts of Rome. If, since 1870, it has been possible for those hills to become thickly populated, it is owing to the fact that a supply of pure drinking water at a high pressure, the *Acqua Marcia*, had been previously conveyed thither.

The condition of the subsoil of the ancient city, composed of alluvial deposits or of rubbish, and impregnated with the organic detritus of many centuries, either directly, or oozing through the walls of badly constructed drains, differs materially from that of the subsoil of the new districts of Rome. The air, contained in the interstices of a soil in such a state, is anything but pure, and its impurity is constantly being intensified in those several portions of the city where the sewers remain such as they were formerly. The consequence is, that whenever a rise in the level of the ground-water, or a diminution of atmospheric pressure in the houses (owing either to general or local causes) drives a certain quantity of this subterranean air into the atmosphere of dwellings, for certain it does not add to their salubrity. As to the waters from wells and from the urban springs of those districts, they must all be considered as doubtful, for they are all exposed to the contamination of poisonous infiltrations from the subsoil, and sometimes even from the drains. Such a condition of things is serious enough under ordinary circumstances, and may become most dangerous during the occurrence of epidemics of typhoid fever or of cholera.

Happily the Municipal Board of Health is displaying great activity in providing remedies for this evil. The new plan of sewerage for the streets and for private dwellings in the ancient quarters, will greatly improve the condition of the subsoil itself, and will preserve the inhaled atmosphere from any impure contaminations. Whilst that is being done, the Municipality has ordered all the wells to be closed, compelling the inhabitants to draw their drinking water from running streams. This measure, which has touched the interests of many, has been greatly found fault with, but I for one consider it most useful.

The experiments which have been made by Professors Marchiafava and Celli, as well as by Dr. Marino, are fully conclusive on that point, inasmuch as not only in the waters from the wells, but also in the waters of many of the urban springs—amongst others the *Acqua Lancisiana*, which had always been considered as perfectly pure—such a quantity of inferior organisms has been found, as to justify the idea that they may easily become the liquid conductors of various infectious diseases.

But, except in the case of a siege, there is an ample supply of good drinking water for the inhabitants of Rome, without their being obliged to have recourse to the subterranean waters of the city. Under the government of the popes, four of the ancient Roman waters, drawn from a distance, were successively brought again into Rome:— The *Vergine*, called *Acqua di Trevi*, because it shows itself at the ancient Trivio; the *Alexandrina*, now called *Acqua Felice*, from the Christian name of Sixtus V.; the *Traiana*, now called the *Acqua Paola*, in honour of Paul V.; and the *Marcia*, called *Acqua Pia*, in honour of Pius IX. The total yield of those waters (if, with Blumenthal, we calculate the quantity supplied by the *Vergine* at only 75,000 cubic metres per day, that is to say, the half of its volume as calculated by Cavalieri) represents a stream yielding 220,000 cubic metres per day. Moreover, the yield of two of these waters—the *Paola* and the *Marcia*—could be easily and sensibly increased. Few cities in the world have, in proportion to their population, such a supply of water, or one that admits of being increased with such facility. Besides, those waters are entirely free from any organic contamination dangerous to health; or may readily be made so, without much difficulty, and without any great expense.

The *Acqua Marcia* is the purest, and is brought into the city from a distance of 50 kilometres, by means of a solid and impervious aqueduct. This water finds its way into Rome on the height of the Quirinal, with such a pressure as enables it to reach the most elevated buildings on the urban hills. It is a very limpid water, always cold ($+ 9°$ at its source and $11°$ in Rome), rich in carbonic acid, which renders it light and pleasant to the taste, and holds in solution a portion of its lime salts. After a period of stagnation, or after being heated, which enables its carbonic acid to free itself, it always leaves a copious deposit of lime salts. These are not in sufficient quantity to render the *Acqua Marcia* hard, inasmuch as it is most easily digested, and vegetables can be properly boiled in it; but, from an economical point of view, they present a serious drawback, for they produce thick incrustations in the distributing pipes, and in the receptacles in which the water is left to boil for a long time.

The *Acqua Felice* also, which is brought to Rome from a distance of 24 kilometres by means of an aqueduct constructed of masonry, and supported by arches, makes its appearance in the Piazza S. Bernardo alle Terme, and is free from organic impurities; but it contains a superabundant quantity of lime salts, which makes it hard; still, even if boiled for a long time, it never produces such thick incrustations as the *Acqua Marcia*, although the latter contains a much less quantity of lime salts. The cause of this curious fact is this: that the *Acqua Felice* contains silica, which, by means of prolonged ebullition, produces a great amount of flakes, around which the lime salts are precipitated, and thus the incrustations formed in the boilers are not very adhesive, and are easily removed. It is for this reason that at the central railway station of Rome they use the *Acqua Felice* for the boilers of the locomotives, or a mixture of the *Acqua Felice* and the *Acqua Marcia*, in preference to the *Acqua Marcia* alone.

The *Acqua Vergine*, which comes through strata of pozzolana, from the great collections of the volcanic basins situated on the Latian hills, bursts forth in the valley of Salone, 12 kilometres from Rome. Thence it is brought into Rome by an aqueduct of masonry, which runs, during the greater part of its length, underground, and which, after a long circuit round the city, enters Rome under the so-called Muro Torto, at a short distance from the Porta del Popolo. It is a limpid water, light and pleasant to the taste, contains but a small quantity of lime salts, and is fit to use for all domestic and industrial purposes. It contains a large proportion of nitrates, which do not proceed from organic matter, but rather from the beds of pozzolana through which it runs previous to springing forth in the valley of Salone. There is no doubt, however, that through the long course which the aqueduct follows within the city, from the Muro Torto to the Fountain of Trevi, much impure organic matter may become mixed with the *Vergine.* For this reason steps are being taken to rectify its course within the city, and to render the walls of its aqueduct impermeable.

The least pure water of Rome is the *Acqua Paola.* Its aqueduct of masonry starts from the ancient Trajan springs on the Sabatian mountains, and winds round the eastern bank of the Lake of Bracciano, before descending into the Roman Campagna. Not only does it convey a portion of the ancient *Acqua Traiana* but, in addition, a sensible quantity of the superficial waters of the Lake of Bracciano, taken in the neighbourhood of the Anguillara. When the waters of the lake are low, there is drawn into the aqueduct a large quantity of the organic detritus floating on the lake, which is carried along as far as the large fountain on the Janiculum. Moreover, before reaching the distributing pipes the *Acqua Paola*, during its course within the city, is subject to an admixture of many other organic impurities. The engineer Vescovali has already proposed to the Municipality to move the *take* of the water of Lake Bracciano from its present spot, and to introduce instead, into the aqueduct, water drawn from a sufficient depth in the lake itself. Neither this undertaking nor the improvement of the urban course of the *Acqua Paola*, need entail any great expense; it is to be hoped, therefore, that the purifying of such a copious stream will soon be accomplished.

As to the modifications which the climate of Rome might undergo through domestic animals, they are considered to be of little consequence. What has been already done, and what is in progress in Rome to obviate the injurious effects of human detritus, will at the same time counteract all danger from contamination of the soil, as well as of the air and water, by the evacuations of the animals accumulated within the city. On the other hand, the ever increasing severity of municipal supervision in the matter of slaughter-houses, veterinary hospitals, the introduction of meat, and the removal of dead animals, obviates the danger of injurious modifications from other sources, which, by means of animals, dead or alive, the climate of the place might otherwise undergo. Outside the city, although the Roman Campagna is essentially a pastoral district, I am not aware of any modification of the climate owing to the animals which are pastured there, unless the not infrequent contamination of the waters in the ditches, by means of the embryos of the *Tænia echinococcus*, be so considered. That very minute tapeworm resides in the intestines of dogs, and sometimes is found in great quantities in the watch-dogs of our numerous flocks of sheep. Issuing from the intestines with the excrement, the proglottis of the *tænia* dies and disappears, freeing the embryos which it contains; and these are easily drawn into the waters of the ditches. Should some of those embryos enter by accident into the stomach of a man drinking that water, they free themselves from their covering, pass into the system, and fix themselves on the liver or other organ of the body. Then they develop themselves, producing what is called a *hydatid*, or *echinococcus*; that is to say, small bladders which, increasing by degrees in volume, become enormous tumours, often causing death. Those hydatids are not uncommon amongst the oxen and pigs of the Roman Campagna, and are also often found in the men who live there. In the Pathological Museum of Rome may be seen a large number of *echinococci* of men, collected by myself during the eleven years I was the Director of the Pathological Institute of Rome; and I am certain that in no other city of Italy could I have collected such a number of specimens, in so short a space of time.

It would, undoubtedly, be a gross exaggeration to consider such an accidental contamination of the waters of the Campagna as a climatical fact. In order to avoid all danger, it would be sufficient to warn the people not to drink the ditch water without boiling it; and not to eat vegetables watered with it, raw, or without first washing them thoroughly in pure water.

Some years ago, a great deal was said and written on the subject of the anthrax of the Campagna of Rome, as if it were an infection spread amongst the cattle and sheep, and thereby proving that our pasture lands were contaminated by the *Bacillus anthracis*. It has now been ascertained as a fact, by scientific investigations, that the anthrax is caused by that *bacillus*, which not only develops itself in the system of infected animals, but germinates and multiplies in the ground contaminated by their evacuations, and by the burying of their carcases. And inasmuch as anthrax is a most dangerous disease, which can be transmitted to man by simple contact with infected animals or their carcases, and probably also by water containing the *Bacillus anthracis*—it was only natural that the reported existence of anthrax in the pasturage of the Campagna of Rome should have created a great sensation.

But the whole of this talking and writing was based upon an egregious error, which was propagated, as often occurs in sanitary matters, by many deluded and some self-interested people.

At that time Pasteur's great discovery of the vaccine of anthrax had been made public, and Pasteur's vaccination had already been tried in several parts of Northern Italy. In some of the inoculated animals anthrax developed itself; but such cases were rare, in comparison with the great number of those in which the vaccination succeeded without producing a similar result. This proved an inducement to extend the process of vaccination to all the places infected with anthrax; and without ascertaining whether anthrax really existed in the Roman Campagna, it was proposed to inoculate with Pasteur's vaccine all the cattle and sheep which pasture there.

Some of the proprietors of the Agro Romano ventured to point out that anthrax did not exist there; that, therefore, vaccination was useless, and, moreover, might be the means of introducing the infection in their territory. They were told by some of the agricultural newspapers that anthrax did exist in the locality, and that their opposition to vaccination was due to their ignorance, and to their systematic objection to all hygienic improvements of the Agro. And no doubt vaccination would have been introduced, had it not been that Professor Celli took part in the controversy, and published a pamphlet to which the municipality of Rome gave a wide circulation.

Celli proved that anthrax did not exist amongst the herds and flocks of the Campagna of Rome, and that what was called anthrax was really the *black quarter* of cattle.

There are, no doubt, in the Roman Campagna some lands where cattle from time to time become infected with this last disease, which is quite different from anthrax, and in fact the Campagna peasants skin the dead animals with impunity and also eat them. Even supposing that it had been clearly proved that Pasteur's vaccination is entirely innocuous, it would, for that very reason, have been a useless expense to have practised it on all the cattle and sheep of the Agro. But, as we already know, that sometimes, even with the best vaccine, the animals inoculated may be attacked by anthrax, there would have been a great risk of infecting the lands of the Agro with a wide-spread and persistent cause of disease. The herds and flocks which pasture there are not kept in stables or in sheds, but are wild, or at least half-wild, and are continually moved from one spot to another. Besides they migrate to the hills in summer, returning to the plains in the autumn. Therefore, should anthrax be once introduced amongst those herds and flocks, the infection of the Agro might easily spread to an unlimited extent; for, besides the direct infection from the pasture grounds caused by the excrement of the sick animals which pasture there, a great danger would arise from the dust of the roads along which the animals travel during their periodical migrations; since this dust, carried about by the winds, might sow the seeds of anthrax at a distance.

Fortunately, the facts adduced by Professor Celli, with the fervour of a sincere and well-founded conviction, had the effect of moderating such senseless delusions, and of preserving the Campagna of Rome from the addition of another source of unhealthiness to those with which nature has already afflicted it, without any intervention of man or beast.

It will be admitted, I think, from what I have stated, that I was justified in asserting from the beginning, that the study of the acquired climates of Rome, whether permanent or transitory, offers no special interest. On that head, Rome may be considered as more healthy than many other cities of Italy or of Europe, and all that has been said to the contrary of late is certainly not confirmed by our sanitary statistics.

It may be freely admitted that, were it not for the malaria, Rome would be the healthiest city in Italy, and that, in spite of the malaria, it can be considered as being amongst the most healthy. Therefore, our paramount interest is concentrated in the study of the *natural climate* of Rome, to which is due the production of malaria.

CHAPTER II.

THE ROMAN SOIL.

IF you were to inquire of a dozen people, where Rome is situated, ten, at least, would reply that it is situated in the midst of a vast plain, containing many marshes which produce the malaria that often infests some parts of the city during the hot season. From our childhood we have been taught, it is true, to call Rome the City of the Seven Hills, but these hills (which, by the way, are more than seven in number) represent to the minds of most persons an elevated island rising out of a level plain. So rooted is that idea, that even in an official publication, sent to the Universal Exhibition of Paris in 1878, the province of Rome is divided into several regions, one of which, the region of the plain, is mentioned as including the whole of the Agro Romano, although the details of a topographical map, annexed to the book, show how far from being a plain is the Agro Romano. It is easy to understand how this strange idea has become so general. In proportion to the great mass of people who inhabit or visit Rome, the number of those, who have explored any portion of the Campagna on foot or on horseback, is exceedingly small. The generality only know the Campagna from what they see out of a railway carriage, or from some vehicle when they drive along the roads leading out of Rome, the principal of which are the Flaminia, the Nomentana, the old and the new Appian Ways, the Tusculana and the Ostiense, which run generally through level ground. The numerous hills, which flank those roads, out of sight, are lost to view, because it rarely happens that houses or trees break the uniformity of the perspective. The unbroken hue of green of the pasture lands, or of lands sown with grains, melts all the outlines, hides the variations of the ground, and leaves the impression of an immense plain, extending from the mountains, which surround the Agro, down to the sea. But, in fact, we have to deal with ground of a most varied description, of which only a fifth part consists of plains. These are confined to the valleys of the Tiber and of the Arno, to the numerous little valleys, which streak in every direction a hilly country; and to the coast line of the Agro. The remainder is occupied by hills, the height of which often reaches a goodly elevation, and we can form a fair notion of the same in Rome itself, where there is the Janiculum with a height of 90 metres above the level of the sea, and immediately outside the city Monte Mario, which is 146 metres high; whilst the banks of the Tiber within the city are only 13 or 14 metres above the sea level.

The boundaries of the Agro Romano, properly so called, are very accurately defined by Nature. To the west and south-west, the sea coast, which extends from Cape Linaro to Torre Astura; from the north to the south, passing eastwards by the Tolfa mountains, the Sabatian, the Simbruini, the Tiburtine, and the Latial mountains. Those limits embrace a vast superficies, which was the theatre of a long and complicated succession of geological events, before becoming the region where so much of the world's history took place.

At the termination of the tertiary period, this portion of the earth's surface constituted the bottom of a sub-Apennine sea, and was formed principally of pliocene soil collected upon beds of miocene. Precedent to, or cotemporaneously with, the conversion of that bottom, the contraction of the terrestrial crust produced in it numerous ripples, which formed the primordial hills of the Agro Romano. Of these hills, consisting for the most part of variously laid stratifications of gravel, sand, and pliocene clays, some have remained uncovered; but in the greater part of them the tertiary soil has been overlaid, entirely or in part, by the eruptions of the Sabatian and Latial volcanoes. Of the former, we have as examples in Rome the Janiculum and the Vatican, and of the latter, the Pincian, the Quirinal, the Viminal, the Esquiline, the Cœlian, the Aventine, the Palatine, and the Capitoline. It is impossible to form an idea, even approximately, of the time which elapsed between the emersion of the sub-Apennine sea bottom, and the volcanic eruptions, which covered it so extensively; but it would seem demonstrated, that, on the Latial side, that interval of time must have been of long duration, as in some specimens collected, principally in the excavations for artesian wells made by the engineer Perreau, were found formations of sweet water between the volcanic eruptions and the surface of the pliocene soil. This seems to point to a geological period in which the latter was covered by swamps or pools, and renders it even probable that a portion of Latium and the Pontine Marshes were united, till the uprising of the great mass of Latial volcanoes.

The hills of the Agro Romano are not all of tertiary formation, whether covered by successive volcanic eruptions or not. During the course of the great Quaternary alluvium, within the deposits of which the Tiber excavated its bed of the historical period, the mass of gravel and sand flowing from the Apennines, drawn down by that enormous alluvial current, heaped itself at intervals on the Agro Romano in the shape of hills. One of these hills may be remarked at a short distance from Rome beyond Ponte Molle, above the fields of Tor di Quinto; a short stretch of that portion of the Via Flaminia, which was turned off towards the hills, in 1849, between Ponte Molle and the *Saxa Rubra*, is cut into it.

The volcanic action, which upheaved that region, has ceased for centuries. It had two principal centres: one, the more ancient and northern, represented by the group of the Sabatian mountains; the other, more recent and southerly, which threw up the mass of the Latial Mountains. Some lingering light of this action flickers through the legends relating to the early centuries of Rome. But at present, of the ancient volcanic activity of the Roman district there remain but the slightest traces on either side of the Tiber. Earthquakes are rare, but, on the other hand, there not infrequently occur seismic movements of the soil, which can only be detected by means of delicate instruments, and are not perceptible to the human senses. Here and there throughout the Agro Romano we perceive exhalations of carbonic or sulphurous acid, and many springs of mineral waters exist, such as the acidulated saline waters of Vicarello, and the sulphureous waters of Stigliano on the right side of the Tiber, and, on the left, the *Aquæ Albulæ* (sulphuric calcareous), and several acidulated waters. In the caves of Canale, on the Sabatian mountains, sulphur is still deposited through sublimation; and in the little lake of the Tartari, below Tivoli, travertine is still being formed, presenting to us, as it were, a microscopic picture of that vast production of travertine, which in former ages took place in various parts of the Campagna of Rome, by means of the deposits left there by an infinite number of springs of mineral water abounding in lime salts.

Amongst the many eruptive craters which were formed during the active period of that vast volcanic formation there were few which emitted materials of a *homogeneous* nature. Those few homogeneous volcanoes were all in the Sabatian group, where they formed trachytic domes, the highest of which is Mount Virginio, which rises to an elevation of 552 metres above the level of the sea. All the other volcanoes of the region are *stratified*; that is to say, they are the product of eruptions, which were accompanied by escapes of gas and of vaporous water, and which issued from channels that maintained the incandescent terrestrial nucleus in direct communication with the earth's surface, as long as each of the eruptive cones continued in activity. When that activity ceased, such communications were closed by the solidifying of the contents of the central channels of the volcanic cones. In some of them the solidification took place when the eruptive matter had filled the central channel as far as the mouth of the crater—as, for example, in the cone of the great Latial volcano, which is called Monte Cavi; but in many others it took place when, between the mouth of the crater and the upper level of the eruptive matter accumulated in the central channel, there was a longer or shorter distance. Thus hollow spaces were formed, some of which, of no considerable depth, became what are now enclosed valleys; whilst others, of a much greater depth, are still, at the present day, lakes.

But, before arriving at the complete extinction of the Roman volcanoes, there elapsed a long period of time, during which the matter ejected from the two volcanic groups was projected in every direction by the tension of the gases and by the vapours of water developed in the central channels of the cones, and covered almost the whole of the Campagna of Rome until within a short distance of the sea.

Until lately the succession of those eruptions was supposed to have occurred thus; it was admitted that the

Sabatian or Sabatine volcanoes existed before the emersion of the sea bottom, and that the tufa formations of the Agro Romano were the product of a kneading of the matter thrown up by those submarine volcanoes with sea water. Moreover, it was admitted that, upon this primitive volcanic bed formed by submarine tufa, there were overlaid, at the north of the Agro Romano, the last eruptions of the Sabatian volcanoes projected into the atmosphere after the emersion of the sub-Apennine bottom; and also at the south of the Agro Romano, the eruptions of the Latial volcanoes, which were thrown up after that emersion, and which were atmospheric from the very beginning. At the present time this theory is untenable. Whilst we have sufficient data for affirming that the Latial volcanoes sprung up later than the Sabatian ones, and were the last manifestation of volcanic action in the Roman district, there are equally cogent reasons for recognizing that the Sabatian volcanoes were atmospheric from their origin, and that their ejections were accumulated on the Campagna when the sedimentary soil had already emerged. In fact, amidst the enormous mass of their volcanic ejections, no marine fossils have ever been found; nor can it be advanced that they are not found because the heat of the volcanic ejections destroyed all traces of pre-existent life. Such a notion is absurd; for it would mean that the matter projected from the craters of Bracciano, of Martignano, of Stracciacappe, or of Baccano, after having travelled under water a distance of 10 or 20 kilometres to constitute the tufa, which covers so many of the Roman hills situated at a great distance from those craters, still retained sufficient heat to destroy, without leaving any traces, even the shells, which it happened to come across in its course.

The incorrect idea, that the tufa of the Roman Campagna is a submarine formation, was suggested principally by the fact, that it constitutes compact masses of great thickness having a uniform appearance, and without any signs of a regular stratification. But the vast cuttings made lately in the Roman hills to dig out the moats of the new forts, have dispelled those superficial impressions. Stratifications of different sorts of tufa have been found placed regularly one upon the other, and these stratified tufas have been also found frequently resting upon perfectly regular stratifications of pozzolana and lava alternately; sometimes, moreover, the lava has been found interlaid between a deep stratum of tufa and the alternate strata of tufa which approach the surface of the hill.

The whole of the sedimentary earths, alluvial deposits, lava streams, volcanic ashes, pumice stone, scoriæ, pozzolana, peperino, and travertine, have made such a geological mosaic on the surface of the Roman soil as is not to be met with elsewhere within so limited a space. The geological maps published hitherto give us an imperfect idea of it, for they are on too small a scale, and were made before geologists had the proper means at their disposal for carrying out so vast a work. Our geological Committee, having been supplied with the necessary means, have completed, on the scale of 1-25,000, a beautiful map of the Agro Romano, which has not yet been published, but of which, the president of the Committee, Giordano, has courteously allowed me to make a copy. Although that map is still incomplete, it shows already 35 different sorts of soils, as entering into the composition of the surface of the Agro. Hence it is easy to understand that such a diversified structure of the immediate subsoil of the Campagna of Rome, does not render the problem of supplying it with agricultural and sanitary improvements less difficult. Any one looking at that map, and remembering how many and various have been the suggestions and plans for the sanitation of the Agro Romano, each considered infallible, that have been put forward during the last 20 years, must regret that it was not made and published before the subject of those improvements was taken in hand. We should have been spared many a delusion, and many absurdities would have been left unsaid. I myself, who in past times have insisted so strongly upon the difficulties created by the complicated structure of the Roman subsoil, did not realize that complication to the full, until after the study of that map.

The geological history of the Roman soil does not end with the modifications caused by the last eruptions of the Latial volcanoes. It has undergone other changes since, in consequence of the action of meteoric waters, and of the alterations which they have produced, not only in its composition, but even in its external features. By degrees, as the geological study of the Agro Romano progresses, various data are being collected, which lead us to believe that some of the tufas are the products of the action of meteoric waters upon pozzolana. It would appear proved, that the prolonged action of water upon pozzolana produces occasionally a natural cement, which is a tufa of a more or less compact sort. In the next chapter I will treat of the immense quantity of meteoric water, stored in the ancient volcanic craters, which permeates the subsoil of the Agro Romano: therefore, if we once allow the possibility of the conversion of pozzolana into tufa, by means of the action of water, we must of necessity admit that such conversion, *in situ*, not only took place near the surface of the soil through the effect of rain falling upon it, and of the streams which flow over it, but in like manner at greater depths through the effect of subterranean infiltrations. And this theory, no doubt, will make it more easy to understand some curiosities of stratification which are frequently found in the cuttings of the tufaceous hills of the Agro Romano.

The enormous quantity of the superficial meteoric water which has overrun that district before our present geological era, besides producing the two great streams of the Tiber and the Arno, produced also a vast number of streamlets, which have cut it up in every direction into ravines of various ramifications. Subsequent to those ancient corrosions of the soil, the region of the Agro has been subjected during the present geological era to many others, to which the hand of man has contributed not a little in the past, and still continues so to do.

Everywhere it happens that the combined action of rain-water and of the atmosphere, upon the soils of the slopes of the mountains and hills, disintegrates their more superficial strata, rendering their constituent parts more movable. Should the incline of those elevated grounds be very steep, the greater portion, or the whole of the disintegrated particles, descends into the valleys by the beds of the streamlets and torrents, or by the landslips which afterwards form, at the base of the mountains and hills, the so-called ejection cones. When, on the other hand, the incline is gentle, the greater portion of the disintegrated soil remains in position, and produces conspicuous strata of vegetable earth, especially when it is held together by the roots of the plants which cover it. But in the Agro Romano there are many hills having gentle slopes, the vegetable soil of which has a great tendency to slide into the valleys. This tendency is due to the small amount of permeability which the subsoil of those hills possesses.

In the Roman hills, the subsoil of which is composed of pumice stone, of sand, of pebbles, or of lava, the rain-water, after passing through the entire thickness of the vegetable stratum, does not remain on the surface of the subsoil. It is quickly absorbed by the pumice stone, the sand, and the gravel, or by the numerous vertical fissures in the lava. But hills of this description are the exception on the Agro Romano. The immediate subsoil of the greater portion of the hills on the Agro Romano is composed of tufa or of clay. The tufas are permeable by water, but in a much less degree than the vegetable soil which covers them; and still less permeable than the tufas during the rainy seasons, is the clay, for when it becomes saturated with water it loses all porosity. The rain water which falls on those hills passes quickly through the vegetable stratum, but is brought to a stand when it reaches the surface of the tufas or of the clays. Hence it is that, as soon as the rain becomes frequent, a large portion of the rain water is upheld by the subsoil, accumulates between it and the vegetable stratum, and forms sheets of water which have a tendency to descend into the valleys, running between the inferior stratum of the vegetable soil and the surface of the subsoil which holds them. Of this fact any one can easily satisfy himself, by travelling on some of the roads in the neighbourhood of Rome. In many places those roads are cut through hills of tufa, and in winter, even when there has been no rain for two or three days, we may often perceive that, whilst the cutting through the vegetable stratum is dry, the cutting through the stratum of tufa immediately under, is dripping with water. That water does not exude from the tufa, but is the watery sheet found between the upper soil and the subsoil, which has been impeded in its descent towards the low ground by the road cutting, and which drips over the vertical wall of tufa.

When the incline of the surface of the tufas and of the clays is sufficiently uniform, the descent of these subterranean watery sheets to the bottom of the hills is unobstructed, and there they form swamps, or produce springs which appear generally about the end of November and disappear at the end of May. But it is very seldom that the slopes of the tufas and the clays are sufficiently uniform to allow of the free flowing of all the rain-waters to the foot of the hills. In most of the Roman hills the declivity is very irregular, and in many points has a different direction to that of the surface of the superincumbent vegetable soil. In this way, on the sides of the hills, are formed subterranean basins in which the rain-waters, filtered through the vegetable soil, accumulate, instead of running down to the valleys, and form small swamps, which have all the characteristics of marshes, and in which marshy plants abound. These little hill swamps are very numerous, and are more frequently found in that part of the Agro which lies to the right of the Tiber;— they are met with at various heights on the sides of the hills, and even near their summits.

It is not surprising that a vegetable soil, which reposes upon a bed so formed, will not adhere strongly to the surface of the subsoil, but shows a tendency rather to slide into the valleys. That tendency is stronger when the subsoil of the hills is composed of clay, because then the watery sheets which undermine the vegetable soil, are more pronounced, and are favoured in their downflow by the slimy polish which the clays of the subsoil often acquire after they have been saturated with rain.

In this way a succession of small landslips are formed in the shape of steps, which are parallel to each other on the sides of the hills, to such an extent that, if this subterranean sapping of the waters be not attended to, the vegetable soil gives way and slides into the adjoining valleys. This mobility of the vegetable soil is less in the tufaceous hills, but man has done all he could to increase it; and the poverty of a great portion of the Campagna of Rome is due to the pains which have been taken to aggravate the not very favourable conditions with which this region has been endowed by nature.

It will be in the recollection of many, that a few years

ago when the public began to take an interest in the plans projected for the improvement of the Agro Romano, a great deal was written in some of the newspapers respecting the wider extension to be given to the cultivation of certain crops, especially of grain. Even the common people caught the idea, and a general subject of conversation was the approaching decrease in the price of bread in Rome, owing to the extended cultivation of grain which was to be introduced in the Agro. There were not a few who busied themselves in propagating this puerile economical idea—heaven knows with what object—asserting that the time had come for giving to the cultivation of that region its proper development. But it must be confessed that the proprietors and tenants of the Agro, though they may have committed many sins of omission in the past, did not commit that one. And it would have been well if they had committed it! If they had confined themselves to sowing seed in the valleys only, and had left untouched by the plough, the hills (which constitute the four-fifths, at least, of the Agro), our poor Campagna would not have been so miserably deficient in vegetable soil, as it is at present. We must remember that the greater portion of those hills is, as already mentioned, formed of tufa, so that when by man's handiwork the vegetable soil, which covered them became loose, the latter, being undermined by the watery sheets mentioned before, was washed off by rain, and precipitated, partly or entirely, into the valleys below, according to the greater or less impetus given to it by the declivity of the subsoil and by the obstinacy of the cultivators. Any person travelling through the Campagna of Rome may frequently see hills, on which the tufa has but a slight covering of vegetable soil, and others where the tufa is laid bare, owing to the vegetable soil, with which it was clothed, having entirely disappeared. On the naked surface there will be found a network of furrow lines;

these are actually the traces left on the tufa by the plough, which cleared away the whole of its productive covering.

The accumulation of these masses of earth, coming down from the hills into the valleys, has raised the level of the latter in a sensible degree, confining at the same time at the base of the hills a quantity of water which formerly flowed off. This is the reason why it often happens that, after walking dryshod through one of the Roman valleys, the traveller of a sudden finds himself sinking into a swamp, when he approaches the foot of a hill, the surface of which is properly drained by a natural drain of sufficient depth. Those swamps are produced by the earth which has slipped down from the overhanging heights, and which is saturated with the waters that formerly flowed away elsewhere, but which, under existing conditions, remain stationary, buried beneath the successive masses of fallen earth. In fact, it not infrequently occurs, during excavations, to find in such spots, at a depth of two metres, and even more, remains of ancient fountains or of ancient basins, which in former days were the recipients of most of those waters at the base of the hills, and regulated their proper flow. Besides, when deep ditches are dug in the Roman valleys, it is not unusual to find extensive stratifications of small fragments of brick, which are parallel with the surface of the valley, at a depth of a metre, or maybe of a metre and a half, below it, and which are the last remains of ancient constructions situated on the hills, that have been washed down into the valleys.

I do not wish to enter into all the details of the action produced by the meteoric waters upon the Roman soil, especially as I should not be able to give a complete elucidation of them without the help of a great number of maps. Any one who feels particularly interested in the question from an agricultural point of view, will find ample information in some of the works which I have published on the subject in the " Proceedings " of the Accademia dei Lincei. It suffices here to have pointed out the most important changes which that action has produced, and still continues to produce, in the soil of the Agro, without a due knowledge of which it is impossible to form a right conception of the hydrography of that region.

CHAPTER III.

THE WATERS OF THE ROMAN REGION.

IF, in order to form a correct notion of the hydrography of the Roman region, we were to limit ourselves to collecting all the data relating to the variations of the flow of the rivers which intersect it, and all the data relating to the quantity of rainfall in each year, we should be as far from arriving at a correct knowledge thereof, as an accountant would be who, in valuing the revenue of an estate composed of personal and landed property were to take account of the former and omit the latter item in his calculations.

The measurements of rainfall made during a period of fifty years at the Observatory of the Collegio Romano give as the average of rain in Rome, 748,$^{mm.}$ 52. No doubt that is too low an average, even for the city of Rome, as the level of a great part of the city is below that of the Observatory, and, consequently, receives a greater amount of rain than is registered by the pluviometer of that Observatory. But, even admitting that the annual average ought to be placed at a higher figure (as, for example, 817,$^{mm.}$ 30, which represents the yearly average for the sixteen years, 1862-77), we should be far from forming a correct estimate of the quantity of water which the subsoil contains. That quantity is infinitely greater than the amount of direct rainfall on the surface of the

Agro Romano, even if that amount were greatly in excess of the hitherto recognized average.

Even during the years of a paucity of rainfall in the winter and spring, and of its entire absence in summer, an immense quantity of subterranean waters may be observed to exist in this region. The rivers which flow through the Agro maintain, after they enter it, a remarkable fulness, even when they have commenced to dry up in their earlier course. At a time when the whole of that region is so arid in summer that cattle cannot exist on it, a great number of subterranean streams continue to feed many perennial springs in the Agro, and to furnish two of the great water supplies of Rome, one of which, the *Felice*, gives 20,000 cubic metres, and the other, the *Vergine*, 75,000 per day at the least. Both those two water supplies well up from the bowels of the subsoil of the Agro to be carried into Rome.

Whence then comes this great volume of subterranean water? From the craters of the ancient volcanoes, formed on the north and south of the Agro in the two chains of the Sabatian and Latial mountains. Those craters form enclosed basins situated at a much higher level than the underlying Agro, all of which collect the rainfall of a much more extensive superficies than that occupied by each of them. Many of those basins do not contain any permanent collection of waters, although in former times some of them were lakes. To the north, the marshes of Stracciacappe (*Lacus Papirianus*) and the valley of Baccano (*Lacus Baccanæ*); to the south, the valley of Ariccia, the camp of Hannibal, the valley of the Molara, and the basin of Pantano, formerly the lake of Castiglione (*Lacus Gabinus*). Others constitute lakes of more or less importance and depth; to the north the lake of Bracciano (*Lacus Sabatinus*), and the lake of Martignano (*Lacus Alsietinus*); to the south the lake of

Albano or of Castello (*Lacus Albanus*), and the lake of Genzano or of Nemi (*Lacus Nemorensis*).

All these basins are the production of stratified volcanoes, and form receptacles which are by no means impermeable; inasmuch as their walls and bottom are in a great measure formed of matter through which water easily percolates—such, for example, as the stratifications of scoriæ, of pumice-stone, of volcanic ashes, of pozzolana, and of the streams of lava. The waters, which collect in those vast basins, descend into the subsoil of the Agro by the simple force of their own gravity, when they proceed from basins which are not lacustrine; but with the addition of a most powerful pressure, when they proceed from craters which are still existing lakes. All these lakes are situated at a considerable height above the level of the sea—the lake of Nemi, 320 metres; of Albano, 295 metres; and of Martignano, 207 metres. The lowest of all is the lake of Bracciano, which is only 164 metres above the sea level. But if we consider that the superficies of that lake measures 5,000 hectares, and that its depth near Trevignano is 500 metres, and consequently the bottom of the lake is 336 metres below the sea level, we shall realize without difficulty how great must be the quantity of water which it injects into the subsoil of the Agro, and the immense force with which it causes it to penetrate therein. And it is truly an injection of water, which those ancient craters produce throughout the whole extent of the Campagna; not only from the effect of their high altitude, but also from the impetus given to the descending waters by the pressure of many atmospheres, caused by the enormous volumes of water accumulated in some of them. The great disruption, which now forms the valley of the Tiber, divides the subterranean waters issuing from the Sabatian mountains from those issuing from the Latial mountains, and the bed of the Tiber is the main collector of both. But still, neither the Tiber nor the small secondary streams of the Roman Campagna, which discharge themselves directly into the sea, collect the entire quantity. They collect enough to maintain themselves in full flow during the driest summers; but a large portion of those waters remain confined within the soil of the Agro, to the great detriment of agriculture and of health.

In fact, those waters, during their course towards the fluvial valleys and the sea, encounter a vast number of obstacles. They penetrate with ease the banks of sand, of gravel, of scoriæ, of pumice-stone, and of pozzolana, as they do also the lava streams, in which are always found a great number of fissures made at the time that the lava shrunk during its solidification. But when in their course underground they meet with banks of peperino, of travertine, of clay, or of tufa, they are arrested during a greater or less length of time, according to the degree of permeability of each obstacle. Sometimes they work their way round them, or beneath, or above, or on the sides, and then continue their downward flow—sometimes they burst forth as springs on the sides, and more especially at the base of the hills. But oftentimes they are unable to overcome the obstacles presented by the subsoil, and consequently remain confined underground; and this is more frequently the case, since the abandonment of the hydraulic works executed by the ancients, and the descent into the valleys of the soil which formerly covered the hills, have multiplied those obstacles, and retain underground a volume of water far greater than that of ancient times.

None of the hydrographic maps, which we as yet possess, are of any use in enabling us to form an idea of the abundance of those subterranean waters. The most recent is Canevari's, annexed to the "Monografia della

Città di Roma e Campagna," which was sent to the Universal Exhibition of Paris in 1878. The map is of the proportion of 1-80,000, and issued by the Pontificial Census, upon which Canevari has marked in blue a great number of spots in the Agro which are marshy. But however numerous may appear the number of places so marked on that map, it is much less than that which really exists; as I proved in 1879, when marking the watery spots of a tract of the Campagna, near Galeria, on a map of 1-15,000. In that sketch of the Agro the map of Canevari gives two marshy spots; on mine are marked forty-five, and I am not sure that that number includes the whole of them. However, even if we did possess (which we are far from doing) a map of the Agro Romano of the dimension of 1-15,000 or of 1-10,000, which accurately defined every one of the thousands of watery spots which exist there, that would not convey a correct notion of the quantity of subterranean water which the Agro contains. As a fact those little morasses only indicate the spots where the subterranean waters rise to the surface, forming marshes more or less extensive; but they are not in any determinable proportion to the quantity of water which is confined in the subsoil.

The hydrographic map of that portion of the Roman region occupied by the city of Rome, which I made in 1884, shows it to us. In it one sees no morasses, for the sewers have eliminated them; and although the two Velabri and the Caprean marsh are marked on it, that is only as a historical record, and to better indicate the places where originally the principal streams of subterranean waters within the city discharged themselves. But those subterranean streams still exist, and one of them, the so-called "Acqua Sallustiana" (*Aqua Petronia*), is well known to all Rome, because, as it falls into the valley of the Tiber by the slope which divides the Pincian from the Quirinal hill, it has to pass beneath a number of houses in the Via del Tritone, where its waters are drawn from wells; and, besides the subterranean streams, the map marks a number of perennial fountains which burst forth from the subsoil of the city, on the sides and at the base of the hills, to the right and left of the Tiber.

I do not pretend to have composed a complete hydrographic map of the subsoil of Rome. Fearing lest I might fall into any mistakes, I have only marked those springs which were ascertained by my friend Rodolfo Lanciani. Besides, I have not traced out the subterranean waters which occupy a great portion of the urban valley of the Tiber, as their limits have not been sufficiently determined. But many persons will remember having seen at work, during a considerable period, a hydraulic machine in the Piazza del Popolo, when the new sewer in the Via Babuino was being constructed. That machine was placed there to keep down the subterranean waters during the progress of the work. If we consider these deficiencies of the map, and remember as well, the great distance which intervenes between Rome and the Latial and Sabatian hills, we readily ask—if we find such a quantity of water in the subsoil of Rome itself, what must be the quantity contained within the Agro Romano, especially in those portions of it which are so much nearer to the ancient volcanic craters than Rome is?

Everything goes to prove that this quantity is enormous. If we travel along the right bank of the Tiber into the Etruscan territory, and proceed through the Campagna towards the Sabatian mountains, we see the external signs of that imposing hydraulic phenomenon always becoming more numerous, especially in the form of perennial springs, which increase in number and volume as we approach those mountains. On the left bank of the Tiber, in the Latial region, those external manifestations are not so numerous, because there, the subterranean waters rarely reach the surface of the soil, owing to the masses of matter which, during the last active period of the Latial volcano, have covered them. But one example will suffice—that of the *Acqua Vergine*—to show us that, on this side of the Tiber as well, those subterranean waters are not lacking. As a matter of fact there is no part of this region where they do not exist.

Many hills to the right of the Tiber, especially those in which thick strata of tufa or of clay lie near the surface, are so saturated, that it is impossible to plant trees on them without providing every hole for planting with a drain. Otherwise the hollows get filled up with water, even when the surface of the soil has been dry for a considerable time. In the valleys and low-lying grounds, filled up as they are everywhere, by the vegetable soil which has descended from the over-lying hills, a great portion of those waters remain confined within the subsoil, and cannot be carried off by the natural emissaries of the valleys, because these are on a higher level than can be reached by the subterranean waters.

If in the former chapter I regretted that, before undertaking the improvement of the Agro Romano, we were not in possession of a geological map of its superficies, approximately exact, with greater reason do I now deplore that it should have been undertaken, without our possessing an approximately exact hydrographic map of the region. The Commission appointed under the law of 1883, for the sanitation of the zone of the Agro nearest to Rome has always insisted upon it, and at present the work is in hand. Perhaps it would have been better if it had been undertaken in the first instance, and that the fundamental law of 1878, for the sanitation of the Agro, had not been passed upon such fallacious notions as are displayed by the imperfect geological map, and by the very deficient hydrographic map, which in that year were officially sent to the Exhibition in Paris as explanatory of the "Monografia della Città di Roma e Campagna," which has already been spoken of. If that course had been followed, the principal aim of a hydraulic sanitation of the Agro Romano would have been placed in the first line of that law, whereas it is not even mentioned in it. And this vital object is: *To draw off the waters from the Roman subsoil, and to cause them to flow into the rivers, or into the sea.* If there be one hydraulic work to be placed in the first category it is surely that :—when the sanitation of the Agro Romano is in question; a vast undertaking at which our ancestors laboured for centuries and centuries, but of which no mention is made in the above-named law.

In it the works which the Government propose to accomplish, are those relating to the regulating of some of the superficial waters, all of which—with the exception of one only, the Almone—are at the periphery of the Agro, and consequently, furthest from Rome.

The *marsh prejudice*—that is to say, the idea that malaria develops itself exclusively in marshy ground—was the principal cause of that error, to the perpetrating of which, the ignorance which then existed respecting the subterranean hydrography of the Roman territory, contributed not a little. In fact, the first book in which the hydrography of the Roman territory is properly described, is Di Tucci's, which was printed after the passing of the law in question. At present the Commission appointed to carry out the law of 1883 for the sanitation of the zone, comprising a radius of 10 kilometres around the golden milestone, is endeavouring to rectify that error; but it is very doubtful whether the fortunes of private individuals will be sufficient of themselves, to secure a complete arrangement of the waters in the subsoil of that zone of the Agro.

It is a question of undertaking works of great magnitude,

and therefore of great expense. The simplest, in appearance, are those destined to clear the subsoil of the valleys from the subterranean waters. And certainly, if the thing could be done in the manner which many imagine to be efficacious—that is, by regulating the streams of water which occupy the "thalweg" of each valley or low-lying ground, and tracing in the plains of the valleys, canals which discharge into these natural collectors—the work would not be so difficult or costly. But experience has proved that such a work is only of use in providing a better drainage for the rain-water, and does not affect in the least the condition of the waters of the subsoil. These retain their former level, and continue to saturate the subsoil of the valleys precisely as formerly. And, inasmuch as the essential point for agriculture, as well as for hygiene, is to procure the lowering of the level of those subterranean waters, it is necessary to have recourse to more efficacious measures than the simple regulating of the rain-waters.

It is necessary to isolate the ground of the Roman valleys, so that no other waters should penetrate therein, except the rain which falls directly upon it. That is the true aim of the hydraulic sanitation of the Roman plains; and, in order to accomplish it, very expensive works must be undertaken. Ditches must be dug along the foot of the hills which flank the valleys and low-lying grounds, of sufficient depth to receive all the waters which, from the sides and bases of the hills, may have a tendency to flow into the valleys. Some enterprising owners, the Piacentini, have undertaken a work of that nature for some years past on the farms of Valchetta and Prima Porta, on the right bank of the Tiber, and have really benefited lands which, until then, were saturated with water, in spite of all the care taken to drain them by ordinary means. Extensive portions of the valley of the Cremera, which formerly were marshy:—the so-called Pantanella, situated almost opposite to the house of Livia (*Villa Liviæ ad gallinas albas*), and a large tract of marshy land in the valley of the Tiber, near the Via di Fiano, have become dried up in consequence of this diverting of the subterranean waters, although made at a great distance from the reclaimed portions. Bearing in mind what I stated in the preceding chapter, respecting the accumulation at the foot of the hills, of the earth which slipped down, it is easy to imagine how exceedingly deep must be the diggings in the soil, to enable these to draw off all the waters which have a tendency to penetrate into the subsoil of the valleys. If we follow with the eye, on the topographical map of the Agro, the perimeter of the hills which flank the valleys, and consider that, in order to accomplish any good result, it is necessary to dig all along that vast perimeter, drains of such great depth, we may easily conclude that it is a question of undertaking and maintaining works of vast magnitude.

But it is a comfort, at least, to be able to say that the result produced by such a work is certain, for it has been put to the test of practical experience; and, therefore, that the problem of the hydraulic sanitation of the low-grounds of the Agro Romano has been solved. The question is one of expense; but questions of simple expense, when the result is certain, are generally solved, sooner or later. From an agricultural point of view the result does not admit of any doubt, and if we cannot say the same as regards the hygienic question, it is to be attributed—as will be explained in the next chapter—not to the deficiency of the means employed for the hydraulic sanitation, but to the doubtful hygienic results produced by it, although in itself perfectly successful.

The worst is this—that the low-lying grounds, in respect of which the problem of the hydraulic sanitation of the Agro Romano may be considered, in a manner, as solved, constitute but a small portion (scarcely a fifth) of the region. The most difficult part yet remains to be solved —that is, how is it possible to relieve the hills of the Agro from the waters which saturate their subsoil? If the larger number of the Roman hills were formed of lava streams, gravel, or sand, or of accumulations of permeable volcanic ejections, the solution of the problem would not be of much consequence; whereas, the greater portion of the Roman hills are composed of volcanic tufas, or of clay, the former scarcely permeable, the latter hardly at all—and sometimes totally impervious. Nature, in some cases, provides these hills with a very efficient drain by means of thick strata of pozzolana, of scoriæ, or of pliocene sand and gravel; but, generally speaking, we have to deal with massive banks of tufa, or of clay, without any natural drainage. Such being the condition of things, the question naturally arises :—is it not possible to obtain an artificial drainage of the subsoil of those hills?

Our knowledge of the geology and hydrography of the Roman subsoil is still too imperfect, to enable me to answer that question in a decided manner. It is true that we have to deal with a region which, during a long succession of centuries, was cultivated by many industrious agricultural populations, and that later on, when Rome was the capital of the ancient world, it became, in a great measure, a pleasure resort. Consequently, an attentive study of the hydraulic operations of the ancients ought to furnish us with valuable hints. But such a study has only been begun since 1878, as it can only be said to have been taken up seriously from the time of the publication of Di Tucci's work, and it is still far from being complete.

We know nothing for certain respecting the attempts which the ancients made to drain the subsoil of the argillaceous hills of the Agro. In 1876, Father Secchi described some galleries excavated in those hills, and which may have been drainage works. They had two lateral walls built of dry masonry, and were covered by a roof of masonry, in which loop-holes were cut. In the inside they were plastered up to a certain height with *opus signinum*—that is, with hydraulic mortar, mixed with pounded bricks, and hence it is doubtful whether they were really drainage works or merely sewers, as Father Secchi was inclined to believe. This doubt no longer exists as regards the drain-works found in the tufaceous hills of the Agro. We know for certain now, that these constituted a vast system of *cunicular drainage*, which sucked in, and then carried off elsewhere, the waters contained in the subsoil of those hills.

From some recent publications I gather that I am considered by many persons, to have been the discoverer of those ancient drainage works. It behoves me to correct that mistake at once. Those galleries, dug in the tufa, had been already seen by Brocchi, by Father Secchi, by Lanciani, and by Canevari, and had been minutely described by Di Tucci before I ever began to study them. Nor was I even the first to point out their use. That had already been done by Di Tucci in 1878. I have no other merit than that of having openly recognized the accuracy of Di Tucci's assertions, when they were looked upon as the lucubrations of a diseased mind, and of having been able to prove by experiment, the drainage purpose for which those *cuniculi* were destined. I must acknowledge, moreover, that 1 should not have succeeded, had I not been assisted by the friendly help of intelligent landowners, such as Alessandro and Tito Piacentini, and by the active collaboration of Colonel de la Penne, director of the works for the new fortifications around Rome.

Those *cuniculi*, or tunnels, are small arched galleries, dug out of the tufa with pickaxes, and have an average height of 1 metre and 50 centimetres, and an average width of 50 centimetres. They formed a network in the interior of the masses of tufa, intersected by wells or shafts, which were used not only for drawing away the excavated materials, and for supplying the workmen with air to breathe, but were used, too, as accesses to the drains for the purpose of penetrating into them to keep them in repair. These shafts are provided with footholds—that is, with holes cut out in the tufa on two lines—which run along the extremity of one of the diameters of the shaft, so that by placing the feet in them it is an easy matter to ascend or descend. The greater portion of those galleries are filled with the deposits which the filtered waters have left there during so many centuries of neglect. These deposits are composed of the finest particles of earth, except in the very rare case where a superficial gallery has its arch in close proximity to the vegetable soil lying above the tufa, or when the arch itself is dug out of the vegetable soil. In the latter case, to prevent the earth falling into the gallery, the arch is backed with flat tiles, which I have found still in place in a little tunnel on the Via Flaminia. Where the slight tufaceous arch, or the arch of flat tiles of those surface *cuniculi* no longer exists, the earth fallen from above has mixed coarser matter with the fine deposits of the filtered waters. When the *cuniculi* are cleared of the rubbish which they contain, the tufa of the walls and of the arches is laid bare, and the marks of the pickaxes used in excavating them are plainly visible. Inside some of the *cuniculi* which I caused to be replaced in their original condition, I found some excavating tools, such as the earthenware lamp, with a ring at the top for hanging, the iron hook on which to hang it, and which was stuck in the tufa according as the excavations progressed, and a short pick, formed by two wedges of iron joined at their ends, which was used by grasping it in the middle. I will relate further on how an occupation, which still exists in some parts of the Abruzzi, enabled me to discover the technic used in those excavations.

These networks of *cuniculi* are to be found in all the tufaceous hills of the Agro Romano, comprising those which are included in the perimeter of the city of Rome, where their subsoil is formed of thick banks of tufa. They are not to be found where the subsoil is formed of thin layers of tufa which rest upon strata of pozzolana. The reason of this is simple: for, as in such cases the subsoil is drained by the pozzolana, there was no necessity for any artificial drainage. An example of this is to be found on the Viminal hill; a great portion of it is composed of very thick banks of tufa, which are entirely honeycombed by *cuniculi*, which were first discovered when digging the foundations of the new Physical Institute; but on the slope upon which the Anatomical Institute is built—that is, on the Via Depretis—the subsoil is composed of a thin layer of tufa, drained naturally by thick seams of pozzolana, and there, no signs of *cuniculi* are to be found. When the banks of tufa are especially thick, the drainage is formed by two or more sets of *cuniculi* placed above each other. On the Viminal, along the Via Palermo, I found two stories of such drains; on the hill where the fort Bravetta is placed, three; and on the Aventine there are four. Those multiplied channels represent on a gigantic scale the so-called "wasps' nests," which our engineers are in the habit of placing under the ground-floor of houses which have no cellaring, in order to draw off the dampness from the subsoil over which they are built.

Sometimes the contents of these *cuniculi* are found dry, and after their removal, the walls and arches of the galleries remain dry also, and they do not resume their former function of drains. That, perhaps, is caused by the changes which have occurred in the distribution of the subterranean waters of the locality during the course of so many centuries. In some of those inactive galleries, the walls of tufa are found covered by a species of natural plaster, formed by minute calcareous incrustations left by the percolating waters, and that has given rise to the idea that their inactivity is due to calcareous deposits of the same nature, which have filled up the pores of the surrounding tufa, rendering it, in fact, impervious. But in many cases the deposits within the *cuniculi* are damp, and when these deposits are removed, the water begins again to ooze through the vaulted roofs and along the walls of the drains. This fact is so well recognized nowadays, that some landowners of the Agro have undertaken the cleaning out of vast stretches of these ancient *cuniculi*, to supply the drinking-troughs for their cattle, with the waters which they drain off.

In the majority of cases, the declivities of the galleries of which this drainage is composed, are arranged so as to draw off all the waters into the valleys. It is probable that the ancients sometimes diverted them, as is done at the present day, into the drinking troughs for their animals, or for other agricultural uses; but generally they gave them free scope to unite with the surface waters, and carried them off elsewhere, together with the latter. This is proved by the mouths of the *cuniculi* being on the sides of the hills, which may be frequently seen by any one who goes through the Campagna; and could be seen even in Rome on the Viminal, above the valley of Quirinus, before the works of the Via Nazionale and the houses of the Via Palermo covered the whole of that side of the hill. In some cases, however, the declivities of the galleries were so arranged as to collect the whole of the drainage waters into a cistern scooped out in the hill, from which they could be easily drawn off by means of wells.

We have a remarkable example of this in the three-storied drain which I discovered during the digging of the moat of the fort Bravetta. The inclines of the *cuniculi* of the highest story carried the drained waters into the galleries of the middle story, and the inclines of these latter conveyed all the waters which they drained, as well as the waters drained by the higher story, into the lowest story, where they entered by means of a single channel, at the mouth of which was placed a perforated piece of lead. The waters flowing from the highest and middle stories, after leaving behind in this filter of lead much of their impurity, mixed with the waters drained by the lowest net of *cuniculi*, and there remained; for these latter were horizontal and had no outlet. Eventually, the waters were drawn off from this sort of cistern by means of two wells. Such was the object of this curious drain, which I discovered when the whole of the contents were cleared away, and the inclines of all the galleries were ascertained. The fact proved that my idea was the correct one; for, as soon as the drains were cleared out, they began to operate, and in a short time the waters filled the lowest story entirely, and the middle one to a great extent.

The conditions of the locality fully explain the object of the work. The hill where now stands the fort Bravetta, between the Aurelian and Portuense roads, forms an elevated table-land, in which no trace of any ancient water-pipes were found, although extensive excavations were made in constructing the moat of the fort. The nearest springs of water are at a great distance, in the underlying valley of the Pisana. The fort is actually built upon the site of a villa of the imperial era, which is supposed to have belonged to a certain Fabius Collio; and there is no doubt that the villa was inhabited by a farming family of some note, for near it there was a cemetery in which were found, in walled tombs, some skeletons, in the mouths of which were pieces of money of the third century of our era. Beneath the ancient house there was a cistern, described by Lanciani, in which were collected the rain-waters. That cistern was composed of short closed galleries, of the same sort as those which formed the lowest stories of the drains which I have just been describing, except that the whole of the interior was covered with a coating of *opus signinum*, to ensure the preservation and the purity of the rain-water collected in it. The cistern supplied the house with drinking water; but was certainly not able to furnish the water required for the domestic animals and the irrigation of the gardens. The fact has proved that this supply was furnished by the drainage ending at a short distance from the villa, and everything tends to show that those drains were made for that express purpose.

Those drains of fort Bravetta, besides furnishing a direct proof of the object of the galleries excavated in the tufa, supply another argument in favour of the notion which I have always entertained, that the Romans were acquainted with and executed works of that nature. No doubt the greater portion of them were carried out by the peoples who preceded the Romans in this region—that is, by the Etruscans, the Latins, and especially the Volsci, in the territory of which latter (which is beyond the limits of the Agro Romano, properly so called) Di Tucci has traced such drains throughout an expanse of 100 and more square kilometres. It is certain that the Romans only continued a very ancient tradition. But some antiquarians still maintain that the silence, which the Roman writers have observed on this subject, is a clear proof that they were ignorant of its existence and of its utility.

I must say that I attach but little value to such an argument. In the first place, it is not certain that such complete silence was observed, inasmuch as no one, as far as I know, has made an exhaustive study of the works of

Cato, Varro, Virgil, Columella, &c., with this special object in view, during the few years which have elapsed since the discovery of the exact purport of these subterranean works, was first made. But even if we admit that none of those writers have ever made any allusion to the subject, this might only prove that they were aware that it was a matter of general knowledge, and so common and widespread, that it was not worth while commenting on it, or undertaking to explain how or why such works should have been made. Moreover, there is one fact that strikes us throughout the whole of Roman history, which is, that whenever mention is made of subterranean galleries, excavated either for military or hydraulic purposes, the fact is stated simply, as if it were the most natural thing in the world; and this, even when historians speak of works of much greater magnitude than those nets of drains. No one alludes as to a wonderful thing, or has handed down to us any technical details respecting the excavation of a much more difficult and imposing work,— the tunnel which, even at the present day, maintains the waters of Lake Albano at a constant level. The military traditions of the Romans assert that the taking of Fidenæ and of Veii was due to *cuniculi* made by the besieging armies, by means of which they were enabled to enter into the fortress (*arx*) of those cities. Titus Livius has preserved this tradition, mentioning, without comment, that those galleries were made; and as to the one at Veii (which, if really executed, must have been a work of great difficulty) he merely observes that the commander of the besiegers, in order to hasten its completion, ordered relays of soldiers, that were relieved every six hours, to work at it. Even Julius Cæsar, who always describes minutely his siege operations, gives no details, when he refers to the tunnel, by means of which he cut off the only drinking water of the besieged at Uxellodunum (Puy d'Issolu, in the department of the Lot), and thereby hastened the taking of the place. He simply states that he cut off the only spring which supplied the besieged with water, by means of *cuniculi*, although it was a very complicated work, as has been shown by Napoleon III.

It consisted of a gallery, averaging 1 metre and 80 centimetres in height, which he began to excavate in shifting soil, and which it was necessary to prop up with wooden scaffoldings, the remains of which are actually in the Museum of St. Germain, near Paris. Then the gallery entered into a bank of tufa; but after a few yards the miners came across argillaceous marl, which obliged them to turn to the left. Beyond the marl they found a hard calcareous rock, and again they had to carry the gallery over the rock. At last they reached the spring, but only after having passed over the higher level of the tufa, so that the last stretch of the gallery had to be dug out of shifting soil, which, as in the beginning, had to be shored up. If during a modern siege such a work had been carried out, who can say at what length it would not have been reported upon, although powder and dynamite would have made the task ever so much easier than in the time of Julius Cæsar? Cæsar does not condescend to dwell upon it for a moment. He merely says that he cut off the spring by means of *cuniculi*, and that is all.

It is easy to understand this indifference if we admit that the art of excavating subterranean galleries was so commonly diffused throughout the agricultural population of Central Italy, that the carrying out of such works created no astonishment when labourers or soldiers from that particular region could be obtained. The readiness with which the Abruzzi labourers, whom I employed in cleaning out the drainage *cuniculi*, found their way about, and at a glance calculated the different inclines, impressed me from the very first time that I undertook those studies, and led me to believe that they must have preserved some tradition of those works. And, in fact, it was so. A lucky accident brought me in contact, in 1882, with a corporal of the Abruzzesi, who came to work in the Campagna of Rome. From that man I learnt that the art of excavating *cuniculi*, similar to the ancient ones of the Agro Romano, was preserved amongst some families of Abruzzo, to one of which he belonged; that in his mountains these galleries are still made for the sake of allowing the pent-up waters to flow; and that, when the tufa is not extraordinarily compact, a digger can push forward a gallery averaging at the rate of a metre a day, a metre and half in height, and 50 centimetres in width; and as the cost of a good day's work amounts to five lire, it is easy to calculate the expense which the excavation of such drainages would involve. Amongst the ancient *cuniculi*, which are to be found in the Campagna of Rome, there are some which are very low, scarcely 90 centimetres in height, and appear at first sight to have been the work of lads. But the corporal explained to me how these were made, for he himself had been employed on similar ones. When the saving of expense is an object, the excavator kneels whilst at work; and is thus enabled to dig out a low tunnel. In such cases he protects his knees by wearing knee-caps.

Should it be admitted that the silence maintained by Roman writers on the subject of this ancient drainage, is of itself sufficient to prove that the Romans were unacquainted with, and did not make use of it, by a parity of reasoning we must deny that the art still exists in Abruzzo, simply because no writer on agricultural subjects makes mention of it.

Let us put aside, however, those historical disquisitions which are beside the question, and stick to facts. The facts prove incontestably and beyond doubt, that the ancients were aware of the existence of a vast quantity of subterranean waters in the Agro Romano; that they were fully alive to the serious detriment which these caused to agriculture; and that, in order to get rid of those waters, they carried out works which were of so extensive a nature that, without fear of exaggeration, they may be designated as colossal. If we carry ourselves back in imagination to the time, when all the deep drainage executed within the interior of the Roman hills was in active operation, when all the rain-waters were collected in the hills and valleys, and when all the springs on the sides and at the foot of the hills were controlled and turned into channels, we may form an idea of the difference between the hydraulic and agricultural condition of things in the subsoil of the Agro Romano which existed in former times, and that of the present day. Formerly the volume of waters, which it contained, was regularly drained off from the Agro, or utilized for the requirements of agriculture, of pasture, and of human life; the vegetable earth on the hills had a greater depth; the level of the valleys was lower and more uniform; whereas, at the present day, the greater quantity of the waters of the Agro is confined in the interior of the hills, or forms marshes on their sides and at their base; the hygrometrical state of the land under cultivation, oscillates between two extremes: excessive humidity during the rainy season, and excessive dryness during the summer; the vegetable soil, which covers the hills, is loosened by the waters with which it is saturated and which flow beneath it, causing it to slide into the valleys below, where it becomes unduly accumulated, burying the waters which spring forth at the base of the hills under its upheaved cones.

If I have succeeded in stating clearly the topographical and geological conditions of the Roman soil in the former chapter, and its hydrographical condition in the present one, it will not require any great stretch of imagination to picture the contrast between the ancient and the actual state of things. And it will be easy to decide which is the better of the two methods of the hydraulic sanitation of the Agro Romano that hold the field. On one side there are those who consider the Agro as a plain, reduced by a long period of neglect, into a similar state as the Lombard plain was, before its hydraulic sanitation was undertaken in the Middle Ages by the Benedictine brethren; and who maintain that the Agro Romano can be completely reclaimed by a proper arrangement of the superficial waters. In other words, that the planting of Eucalyptus trees, the rectification of some water-courses, and the drying up of certain marshes, are sufficient means for restoring the hydrographical conditions of the Agro to the same state in which they were in ancient times. On the other side are those who, recognizing the curious complications which are met with in the configuration, the structure, and the hydrography of that region, as well as those which the destructive work of man has added, hold that the hydraulic sanitation of the Agro Romano constitutes a problem most difficult to solve. They do not even attempt to say that a complete hydraulic sanitation of the Agro Romano can be obtained with any certainty, but confine themselves within the limits of asserting that, in order to obtain useful results, it is necessary *to work upwards, step by step, to that point from which, during the lapse of so many centuries, the downward course has been in progress,* as was said by the Marchese Raffaele Panto, one of the most distinguished Italian hydraulic engineers, who, during the latter years of his life, was lovingly occupied with matters relating to the Campagna of Rome.

Unfortunately, we are still very far from knowing the length of the road which we have to travel. By the recent geological and hydrographical studies some steps in advance have been made; but a much more profound study will be necessary, before any one can venture to say that the subject of the complete arrangement of the waters of the Agro Romano, can be discussed with a full knowledge of the matter.

CHAPTER IV.

THE ROMAN MALARIA.

In every country whenever attempts are made to obtain a correct knowledge of the existence or intensity of the effects of malaria in any given district, a great many difficulties have to be overcome before arriving at the exact truth. Inasmuch as malaria is a production of the earth, and that land constitutes property, the commercial and taxable value of which, varies according to the degree of fertility and salubrity with which it is invested, many interests have to be dealt with; the aim of some being to deny or to minimize, and of others to affirm or to exaggerate the facts in connection with this baneful production of the soil. If this happens in a greater or less degree when only minor interests are at stake, we may imagine what occurs when the malaria of Rome is in question. Here we have not only to deal with economical interests conspiring in different ways to hide or to alter the truth; but besides with an agglomeration of religious, social, and political interests, which in their various conflicts have often made use of the Roman malaria as an offensive or defensive weapon, according to circumstances. It is sufficient to bring to mind what was said before 1870 and since, upon the potency of the Roman malaria in order to dissuade the Italian Government from making Rome the capital of Italy; to understand how here, more than elsewhere, it is difficult to prosecute researches after the truth.

Political passions have gone even so far as to falsify the history of the Roman malaria, and it has been asserted by some, with a view of displaying their liberalism, that it did not exist in ancient times, but was devised by the Popes. Only a few years ago, Pelletan gravely wrote that the Popes maintained the desolation and unhealthiness of the Agro Romano, in order that the monuments and beauty of Rome might strike the stranger entering it with greater effect after travelling through the former. When a not unknown writer allows himself to make such ridiculous mis-statements, it is a sign that the notions prevalent in the world respecting Roman malaria, are such as to render imperative, an accurate examination of the historical facts which bear upon the subject, and the more so, that it is impossible to form a correct conception of the actual state of things, and still less of what remedies ought to be applied to it, if we undertake the discussion starting from a distorted notion of its origin.

I have no hesitation in affirming that the malaria here dates back to a most remote age, and that probably this region was malarious when the first colonies were established in it. I put aside the tradition, according to which, primitive Rome (*Roma quadrata*) was founded on the Palatine because it was a salubrious spot in the midst of a pestilential district; for, although such a tradition was accepted by Cicero, it may justly be objected, that legends relating to such remote ages ought not to be received as historical documents. But there is one thing which fully bears out my statement, and that is, that from the earliest days of Rome a special worship of the Goddess Fever was instituted. All the peoples of ancient classical times have shown a common tendency to personify the great enemy of their new colonies—the malaria. Each race personified it in its own manner, and according to its particular genius; the Pelasgi represented it as the

Lernean Hydra overcome by Hercules; the Greek colonies of Pœstum, of Sibaris, of Agrigentum, and of Selinunte, as a wicked demon, or a monster that devoured men. The Latins, less imaginative, did not convert into a myth the cause of the unhealthiness of the region where they settled; they simply considered the effects of it, and, looking upon the effect, and the cause which produced it, as one, instituted the cult of the "*Dea Febris.*" To appease the fury of this divinity they erected temples in her honour, and instituted a worship which religious tradition carried on, even after the notion of natural things became less vague, and the struggle of men against the maleficent agency of malaria assumed a more practical form.

But even after the condition of the Roman territory had become ameliorated by cultivation and hydraulic works, many monuments of which still exist, it continued to produce malaria, and historical records of this are not wanting. Titus Livius relates that in the 5th century of Rome (year 413 U.C., 339 B.C.) during the Samnite war, Capua, which had surrendered by capitulation to the Samnites, was retaken by the legions, and that after the victory the legions mutinied. The reason for the mutiny was this: they thought it strange that people who had not been able to defend the productive soil of the Agro Campano should return to enjoy it, and asked "if it was just, that they themselves, who had had their health ruined during the war, should return to cultivate the ungrateful and pestiferous soil of the Agro Romano, or to remain in Rome at the mercy of the usurers?" Three centuries later, under Augustus, Horace deplores the mortality caused by fever during the month of October, which, in his opinion, "*adducit febris et testamenta resignat.*" Tacitus narrates that in the year 69 of our era there was a great mortality in the army of Vitellius, because they were encamped on the Vatican, which, to this day, often produces malaria in hot and damp seasons. The Emperor Titus died in the year 81, soon after his arrival at his villa Cutilia, on the Sabine hills, from a fever caught during his journey thither across the Roman Campagna. And again in the year 96, Nerva carried out some improvements, which Frontinus praises as works tending to purify the bad air of Rome.

Searching through the Latin authors, it would be easy to multiply historical proofs of the persistency of the malaria in the region of Rome, during the long interval between the establishment of the first colonies which have left some records of themselves, and the second century of the Christian era. In that century, which is that of the Antonines, it would appear that the malaria was reduced to a minimum, because, amongst other things, we know that Marcus Aurelius (161—180, A.D.) sojourned, even in summer, at Bottaccia, near Castel di Guido, which is an unhealthy spot now. It is impossible, however, to say that it had entirely disappeared; for that indifference to living on the Campagna of Rome during a dangerous season, proves no doubt, that there was not the fear of incurring the same risks then, which exist now, but it is not sufficient to prove that there was no danger of catching fever there in those days.

We are not able to judge of the manner of thinking and feeling of the ancients on that point, by the standard of ideas which is prevalent amongst us at the present day. Had they been afflicted with the health mania, which for many years has taken hold of the people and the Government in Italy, and which, in 1884, made us appear so ridiculous in the eyes of all civilized nations, during the visitation of cholera, they would never have settled in Latium, nor would they have performed the mighty deeds which they accomplished. But neither they, nor their distant descendants of the Middle Ages, and of the time of the Renaissance, had any of these fads in their heads; and would most certainly have laughed at the idea of changing their civil, military, and social life, through fear of catching some fever. It is true that they were able, both at the former and latter periods, to resist more successfully than we moderns, the attacks of malaria, because, as will be seen in a later chapter, the absence of those sure specifics against such attacks enabled human races in former times to offer a more obstinate resistance to malaria, whereas the general use of them at the present day, renders this resistance much more feeble. And besides, it is probable that they did not always know how to trace back to their original cause the most dangerous attacks of malaria, as many of these do not in the least resemble attacks of common intermittent fever, and often, even now, are attributed to other causes, by those who have not had a long experience in places where virulent malaria is prevalent.

It is not at all unlikely that many secret assassinations and many instances of poisoning, recorded as such in the chronicles of ancient Rome, were purely and simply cases of death caused by deadly malaria, because we have seen many errors of the sort interwoven in the Italian history of the last four centuries, and accepted as true. There are, in fact, many reasons for believing that the final catastrophe which befell the Borgias in 1503, instead of being due to a mistake in the administering of a poison prepared for some other persons, was caused simply by an attack of a malignant fever which killed the Pope, already an old man, but which Cæsar Borgia, young and robust, was able to overcome. Alfieri's tragedy, "Don Garzia," has no foundation in fact; we know now for certain that the two sons of Cosmo I. of Tuscany, Cardinal John and Don Garzia, died at Pisa of fever, contracted whilst they were hunting in the Tuscan Maremma. But in Tuscan stories we are told of a fratricide, and then of the murder of the culprit by a furious father; and this legend was handed down from century to century, till the time of Alfieri, who made it the subject of his tragedy.

The deaths of Francesco I. de Medici and of Bianca Cappello were due to a malarious fever, which they took during a great hunt in the environs of the Poggio a Cajano; and the story of the cake prepared by Bianca to poison her brother-in-law, eaten first by the Grand Duke by mistake, and then by the wife in despair at seeing the failure of her scheme, is a pure invention. Even at the present day it is not unusual to hear of poison being suggested, when an attack of deadly fever carries off some great personage. For instance, a few years ago, whilst in Germany, I heard it stated in a company of educated people, that Cardinal Franchi, the Secretary of State of Leo XIII., had died from poison. Some newspapers had made the assertion, and many people believed it. There was a difference of opinion, only as to the perpetrators of the crime. Some said that the Cardinal had been poisoned by the Jesuits, because he was too liberal in his ideas; and others by the Italian Liberals, because he administered the affairs of the Holy See too successfully.

In default of trustworthy historical documents, it is not easy to decide, at a distance of so many centuries, whether at the commencement of our era, when the prosperity of Rome had reached its apogee, our ancestors had succeeded in entirely freeing the Agro Romano from malaria. But even if that be admitted, it could not be a complete extinction of the baneful production, but a suspension of its pernicious effects, which lasted as long as the works undertaken for that purpose continued to operate. As soon as these were abandoned, the immunity derived from them also ceased, and by degrees the malaria returned to infest the region from which it had not been expelled, but only reduced to a state in which it had lost its deadly power, through the accumulated efforts of centuries. In order to understand this phenomenon, as well as the actual state of things,—the improvements already effected in the interior of the City of Rome since 1870, and those which are hoped for in the Agro Romano,—it is necessary to form a correct notion of the nature of malaria, and of the conditions under which it is produced.

The first thing to do is to clear our mind of a prejudice, ingrained in doctors, as well as in those who are not of the medical profession, to which is to be attributed an infinite number of incorrect theories, seriously broached as being scientific, and what is worse, a vast amount of expenditure out of the public purse, which has turned out useless and often injurious. It is a most difficult prejudice to eradicate, and no one is more conscious of it than myself, who in 1860 had the luck to receive a severe lesson on the subject, and still did not succeed in ridding myself of it till much later. The prejudice of which I am speaking is this, *that malaria is produced only in stagnant waters through the putrefaction of the dead animal and vegetable organic matter which they contain.* This putrid-marsh prejudice pervades the whole natural history of malaria, and provides the terms usually adopted in books to explain everything relating to malaria. It was considered a step in advance to call "marshy miasma" the morbid ferment which determines malarious infection; whereas it was a step taken backwards, as is always the case, when an erroneous scientific idea is substituted for the teachings of popular practical experience.

The inhabitants of Italy, who unfortunately are the most experienced on this subject, use the word malaria (bad air) to indicate the specific agency of intermittent and pernicious fevers. Italy possesses the unenviable privilege of having given this word to the world, by which it has been universally adopted. It has, at least, the merit of not prejudging any opinion regarding the nature of that specific agent. It indicates an undoubted fact only; which is, that that agent pervades the air which is breathed, and renders it capable of infecting the human organs, into which it introduces itself by the respiratory tubes. The mind is not occupied by any preconceived notions respecting the origin and the nature of such agency, and is consequently free to devote itself to the necessary researches relating to the same, without the trammels of prejudice or bias.

When one talks of "marsh miasma," and falls into the habit of thinking of that specific unwholesomeness of the air as only proceeding from a marshy origin, the mind of the thinker is from the first confined within a certain groove, and cannot leave it. And inasmuch as that groove is a wrong one, it is natural that error should be heaped upon error in a fatal sequence. The supposition is, that malaria is generated in stagnant water, in which organic matter becomes putrefied. Consequently it is inferred that it is produced only in marshes, in stagnant pools, in soaking tanks of hemp and flax, in swamps, in rice beds, and in places where salt water mixes with fresh water, and in which a vast quantity of organisms, which cannot live in such a mixture, die and putrefy. Logically, it would be necessary to admit, that in every place so circumstanced, malaria will always develop itself whenever the putrefaction of which we have been speaking, takes place in water under the above conditions. Facts, however, prove the contrary, for in every quarter of the globe exist marshes, stagnant pools, soakings of hemp and flax, swamps, rice beds, and mixtures of salt and fresh water, which in the hot weather exhale a great quantity of putrid productions, without engendering any sort of malaria. But when we get upon the hobbyhorse of a particular theory and wish to maintain it at all costs, we always follow the simple plan of ignoring all the facts which militate against it, and only recognize those which support it. Such negative proofs therefore are not to be taken into consideration. It very often happens, however, that people find themselves in places where malaria rages, but where there are no signs of pools of putrid water, and, in order to escape from the difficulty, diligent search is made in the maps to see whether some such pools may not exist in some adjoining locality. And should one be found, never mind at what distance, people immediately infer that the malaria generated in that hotbed, is carried by the winds as far as the places where there are no such stagnant waters; and generally the assertion is made, without any trouble being taken to ascertain whether the appearance of fever in these latter places, coincides with the arrival of atmospheric currents from the direction of the former. But sometimes even this explanation cannot be given, when it happens that no stagnant pools are found anywhere along the region over which the winds must blow previous to reaching the places where malaria exists. In such cases it not seldom happens that, rather than admit the existence of malaria contrary to the accepted rules, its existence is doubted. I, myself, was once led into a similar sin through my school prejudices (a sin which the Church numbers amongst those which call for vengeance from the Lord), and denied an ascertained truth, in order not to prove myself unfaithful to an erroneous tradition. But I make a clean breast of it now, that others may profit by the lesson which I learnt so many years ago.

During the march which Garibaldi's small army made in July, 1860, on Milazzo, along the northern coast of Sicily, the regiment in which I served as a Major had to encamp one night at Cape Orlando. We arrived during a splendid moonlight night upon the upper slope of a hill which overlooked the Æolian Isles, and on that slope the camp was to be pitched. The Sicilian guide advised the Colonel not to encamp there, as the place was malarious. The Colonel was astonished to hear that malaria existed in such a beautiful spot and at such an elevation, and sent me to find out if such were the case. I questioned the Sicilian guide, and having ascertained from him that in the neighbourhood there were no marshes, no swamps, no rice beds, no stagnant pools, &c., I pronounced the man to be mistaken, because situated as we were, with the hill behind us towards the south, and with the sea before us towards the north, there could not be any drift of malaria existing elsewhere, and such a dry and elevated ground could not possibly produce any. But that ground did produce it, and so badly, that in the morning, after having pitched our camp there, several of the men were attacked with intermittent fever. Naturally such an incident shook my faith in the marsh theory, but it did not suffice to drive it entirely out of my head, and a long study was necessary, but above all a long intercourse with the inhabitants of the different malarious regions of Italy, before I succeeded in entirely freeing my mind from that prejudice.

Malaria is produced in the earth and not in water, a peasant of the neighbourhood of Palermo told me many years ago, when the sanitation of the marshes of Mondello was under discussion. And that is the correct formula. The *sine quâ non* condition of the production of malaria, is the existence of the malarious ferment in the earth. In places, which do not hold that ferment, there may exist every form of marshy ground and every sort of putrefaction in dead water, but malaria is not generated. Water is no doubt an indispensable element of the fatal product, because if the malarious soil is not kept damp during the hot weather it is unable to produce malaria.

Consequently, all other conditions being equal, malarious regions, where stagnant water is found, are justly considered as the most infected, because there the humidity indispensable to the production of malaria is never absent, even in the driest summers. But also, it is not necessary that there should be swamps of any kind, in order that malaria should exist. If such were the case, Italy would be a much more fortunate country than she is, since at least two-thirds of her soil which produces malaria would be perfectly healthy. A very small amount of humidity is sufficient to stir the noxious production in places, where the germs of the ferment exist in the earth, and we often find plains, hills, and mountains, the surface of which is perfectly dry in summer, but which nevertheless give out malaria, owing to the small amount of humidity which their immediate subsoil contains.

It may happen, on the contrary, and often does happen, that the accumulation of water on the surface of a malarious soil prevents the specific poisoning of the atmosphere which lies above it. This occurs whenever the water completely covers the infected soil. A sheet of water interposed between the soil-producing malaria and the atmosphere which covers it, acts as an obstacle to the malarious germs, and protects the air of the locality from the specific poisoning. We see this every year, in those districts of Italy where there are numerous rice-beds made in malarious ground. As long as the rice is in vegetation, and the whole of the surface of the rice-beds is covered with water, the rice-beds do not produce malaria, even during the prevalence of the greatest heat. The breaking out of fever takes place later on, when the water is drained off in order to harvest the rice, and the surface of the beds comes into immediate contact with the atmospheric air. Also, in marshes situated in malarious grounds, it sometimes happens that the production of malaria becomes suspended, because the water is so exceptionally abundant during the hot season that it maintains an uniform covering over the whole of their surface, and keeps itself at a certain height on the banks. In that water the usual marsh putrefactions are to be found, but malaria is not produced; it does, however, burst forth as soon as the level of the water decreases, so as to lay bare smaller or larger stretches of the bottom or of the ridges. Art has profited by these hints given by Nature itself, and everywhere are to be seen examples of the sanitation of malarious lands obtained by water. I could quote a great number of instances, but I will confine myself to two only, taken from Italy, not to go too far afield—and these are supplied by the lakes of Mantua and by the lake of Avernus.

Mantua is situated in the midst of a malarious region, as the different armies, which have laid siege to it during the hot season, have learnt to their cost. The valley of the Mincio, as it approaches Mantua, widens out, and forms the higher lake, and afterwards divides into two branches, one into the valley of Paiolo to the west, and the other to the east, where the Mincio forms the middle and lower lakes. The waters of the higher lake are always maintained at the same level, by a dyke stretching from the heights of Belfiore to those of S. Giorgio, which is furnished with sluices, some of which enable the valley of Paiolo to be flooded in time of war, whereas others are always in operation to regulate the height of the water in the lake, and to turn off into the middle and lower lakes greater or less volumes of water. This last lake (the lower) has a natural outlet in the Mincio which, flowing in a more confined bed, empties itself into the Po below Governolo. The waters of the lower lake keep pretty much on the same level as the Po. Long experience has proved that, when the waters of the Po reach the height of 1·50 metres above zero on the hydrometer at Governolo, the ridges of the lower lake are submerged, and fever does not show itself in Mantua; whereas, when the level of the Po falls below that point, and the ridges of the lower lake begin to be uncovered, an outbreak of malaria follows. In order to remedy this calamity they used, till 1848, a movable dam erected during the twelfth century near the outfall of the Mincio into the Po. This dam was furnished with sluice-gates, which were closed whenever the level of the Po fell below the above-mentioned point; so that the waters of the Mincio were able, even when the Po was at its lowest, to cover the ridges of the lower lake. The destruction of that dam, for military reasons, in 1848, brought about, during the succeeding years, a series of malaria epidemics in Mantua whenever the waters of the Po, and consequently of the lower lake, became shallow. Hence the persistent demand of the Mantuans, since 1866, for a re-establishment of the dam at Governolo, in order to prevent the renewal of the periodical laying bare of those malarious ridges of the lower lake, which are so detrimental to their city.

Analogous facts are to be found in many parts of Italy, where the malarious regions are in the proximity of the sea, and where such regions are exposed to be alternately submerged and laid bare whenever the sea, raised by the tide or by wind, reaches an unusual height, and afterwards recedes, leaving bare larger or smaller tracts of malarious ground. After such occurrences there is a great increase of malarious emanations given out by the soil, and sometimes even a renewal of the malarious production on lands, where it had ceased for a while. Bernardino Zendrini, a hydraulic engineer of great and well-deserved celebrity in the last century, sought to prevent this calamity, by applying the system of the movable dam of Governolo in the reverse way—that is, by building sluices on the strand, which closed when the sea was high, and opened when it retreated. By this means the sea-water did not penetrate into the malarious lands, and the dangerous alternation of their being submerged and laid bare was avoided.

The practical utility of this defensive work is manifest in many parts of Italy, especially in Tuscany; and some medical schools have adduced it as a proof of the origin of malaria from the mixing of salt and fresh water, which, by this means, is obviated; without reflecting, that were this the case, malaria would be developed in every locality where such a mixture takes place (which is not true), and especially in the city of Venice, where there is a constant mixing of fresh and salt water in all the canals which intersect it in every direction. The reason of the utility of Zendrini's system is simply the one which I have already explained. In fact, that system is only successful when the fresh waters which flow towards the sea, and which are held back by the sluices when they are shut, are not sufficient to submerge the malarious ground. When, on the contrary, the fresh waters are abundant, and produce alternately submersions and emersions of the malarious soil, the system of Zendrini may prove dangerous. This happened with the lake of Orbetello, which, when it was attempted to cut off its communication with the sea, under the Zendrini system in 1860, produced so much malaria in Orbetello, that the Government had to interfere, and restored the former free communication with the sea.

The sanitation of the marsh of Averno has been effected by digging out the bottom and heightening the ridges, so as to convert it into a lake constantly filled with water. That operation has been most successful; and it is to be hoped that similar operations will be undertaken with swamps in which the same conditions exist, instead of having recourse to the plan of drying them up, which seems to be more in favour at the present day. This last system may lead to lamentable disappointments. As a matter of fact, when the sheet of water which covers the bottom of a malarious swamp is drained off, nothing is gained, if the subsoil of the desiccated surface remains in a state of humidity during the heat of summer. A contrary result to that sought for is obtained, because the desiccation of the surface brings into direct contact with the atmosphere a large extent of malaria-producing ground.

Malaria-producing grounds are found in every part of the world. Except in those regions situated beyond the Polar circles, there is no portion of the terrestrial globe known, where, either in a greater or less degree, this dire production may not show itself. And what is more distressing, there is no known quality of soil, except compact rocky formations, which, *à priori*, can be said not to be capable of generating that infection of the local atmosphere. The production of malaria occurs in soils of the most varied description, and situated in every sort of locality—in low-lying places well supplied with water and organic matter, as well as in hilly and mountainous sites, apparently dry and deficient in organic matter; in volcanic lands, as well as in the sedimentary ground of every geological period; and even in soil composed of quartziferous sand, as McNally and others have observed in the East Indies. Next to the septic ferment, the malaria ferment is, amongst all the morbific ferments, the one which is most widely diffused throughout the world, and which most readily finds conditions adapted to its development and to its dissemination.

What is this ferment?—I will not undertake to give a long explanation of its nature; because, although the study of it has already made great progress, it is not yet completed. But it may be well to say something on the subject, in order to arrive at a better understanding of the questions relating to the Roman malaria.

The notion that this ferment is occasioned by a living organism was held in ancient times, and is not an outcome of modern parasitic theories. From Varro (who thought that malaria was engendered by invisible living animalculæ floating in the air), until our own days, that idea has gained ground, at different intervals, amongst hygienists. Independently of the different reasons which induced Rasori, and, later on, Henle, to formulate the doctrine of the *contagium virum* of infections (long before the existence of morbific ferments had been revealed by the microscope), there were, as regards malaria, special circumstances which necessarily led the minds of people to that conclusion, even in the most remote times. Some of those circumstances are such, as to strike any unprejudiced observer, and to deserve a moment's attention.

How, for instance, can any one maintain that malaria is a product of the chemical reactions which take place in the interior of the soil, when we see that this morbific ferment is always the same, whatever may be the composition of the soil from which it emanates? As long as the marsh prejudice was recognized, this identity in every malaria region could be explained easily enough. No one can question the fact that in every part of the world, the putrid decompositions of the organic matter contained within the marshy lands take place, as soon as the beams of the sun raise the temperature of the soil to the degree required for those chemical processes; and that consequently the *chemical ferment*, or the *mephitic gas*, to which the morbific agency was attributed by the paludal theory, could be developed everywhere in exactly the same manner. But since it has been ascertained that malaria can be produced in non-marshy grounds, and in soils of the most varied composition, the constant identity of this product is no longer chemically conceivable; whilst it is easily understood, if we allow that malaria is a living ferment, which finds conditions favourable to its existence and its multiplication, in soils of the most different natures, as is the case with thousands of other organisms far superior to the rudimentary ones which constitute the living ferments.

The same thing may be said of the increasing intensity of morbific production in malarious places which have been abandoned to themselves. This fact is proved by numerous historical instances, especially in Italy. Many great Etruscan and Latin cities (Rome itself) sprang up in the midst of malarious regions, and reached a high degree of prosperity. Amongst the causes which contributed to the triumph of man over the unhealthy nature of those places, must be placed in the forefront the works of sanitation, which, in the course of centuries, diminished the obnoxious production, but scarcely ever extinguished it completely. After those works were abandoned, the production of malaria began at once to reassume greater proportions, and to increase progressively to such a degree as to render many of those places uninhabitable. During the dominion of Rome, that happened in a great portion of Etruria, after it was conquered and devastated; and in many parts of Magna Grecia and of Sicily. From the fall of Rome until the present day, the same phenomenon has been reproduced in the Agro Romano. There are, in fact, in the Campagna of Rome, certain localities in which, in times not very distant, it was possible to reside, and which at present it is impossible to inhabit during the hot season. In many of those localities, the physical conditions of the soil have not undergone much change for centuries; consequently, it is impossible to attribute so enormous an augmentation of malaria, to any increase of its mineral production, caused by a progressive alteration of the chemical composition of the soil. But if it be admitted that malaria is caused by a living organism, the successive generations of which infect more extensively the region which holds it, the interpretation of the fact presents no difficulty.

There are, moreover, some peculiarities in the local charging of the atmosphere with malaria, which cannot admit of any other explanation. If the malarious miasma were composed of gaseous bodies emanating from the soil, or of chemical ferments formed in the soil, and drawn up into the atmosphere together with watery vapours, the malarious load of the atmosphere ought to reach its maximum, during those hours in which the ground receives the greatest amount of heat from the rays of the sun, and in which the evaporation of water and all chemical processes attain their greatest intensity. But what actually occurs is quite different. The malarious charge of the atmosphere is less strong during the midday hours than at the beginning and the end of the day; that is, after sunrise, and more especially after sunset. Now it is precisely during those two periods of the day, that the difference between the temperature of the lower strata of the atmosphere and the temperature of the surface of the soil is greatest, and that the currents of air which ascend vertically from the soil into the superincumbent atmosphere, are strongest. If malaria consists of solid particles of minute specific weight contained in the soil, we readily comprehend how their ascension into the atmosphere would take place, particularly during these two periods of the day.

All these facts, which can be easily verified, if the subject of malaria be studied on the spot, and without any preconceived notions, explain the tendency which has always existed, to attribute this specific poisoning of the air to a living organism, which multiplies itself in the soil; and they also explain the zeal with which so many hygienists have endeavoured to prove its existence. Unfortunately, the experiments undertaken to arrive at this scientific proof remained abortive for a long time, owing to the marsh prejudice, which induced the investigators to give their attention solely to the inferior organisms which inhabit the marshes. Amongst these organisms they especially studied the Hyphomicetes, which had already acquired a prominent place in the pathology of the skin; and every one's attention was concentrated for a time upon the aquatic algæ, without ascertaining whether the species of algæ, which were said to be malarious, were to be found in all the malaria-producing marshes, or whether they were capable of living as parasites within the human body. Thus it has happened that each observer has indicated as the cause of malaria a different variety of algæ; each one asserting that malaria was caused by the particular algæ which most abounded in the mud of that special swamp that he had examined. In fact, Salisbury singled out the "*Pamella gemiasma*," which Lanzi and Terrigi have discovered in many places where there is no malaria, and which is not to be found in any of the malarious marshes of the province of Rome. Balestra selected other algæ, the exact species of which nobody has determined; Bargellini, the "*Palmoglea micrococca*"; Safford and Bartlett, the "*Hydrogastrum granulatum*"; and Archer, the "*Chtonoblastus aeriginosus*." Amongst all those species not a single one has been proved to be parasitic; and as to the last two, it can be boldly affirmed, without seeking for any other proof, that they are incapable of producing a general infection of the human body, as the diameter of their spores and filaments is greater than the diameter of the capillary blood-vessels.

It was only in 1879 that Klebs and I, after having

freed ourselves from the marsh prejudice by a long course of preparatory studies, undertook, in collaboration, the examination of a large quantity of malarious earth—marshy and non-marshy. We adopted the method of procuring a fractional culture of the minute organisms contained in that earth, making subsequent experiments upon animals with the last products thus obtained. We ascertained that the malarial ferment is constituted by a living organism which infects many varieties of soil, and multiplies in the human body. Later observers (and especially Prof. Celli) have succeeded in demonstrating, that this parasite attacks directly the red blood-globules and destroys them, causing them to undergo a series of very characteristic changes, which render certain the diagnosis of the malarial infection.

The controversy, still extant, about the animal or vegetable nature of this very minute parasitic being, does not interest the hygienist. The essential thing for him to know is, that he has to deal with a living ferment, which can flourish in soils of the most varied composition, and without the presence of which, neither marshes nor swamps of putrid water are capable of producing malaria.

It would be wrong, however, to believe that all soils which contain this ferment poison the local atmosphere. Popular experience, some of the modern scientific investigations, and the results which occur whenever extensive diggings are made in a soil that was malarious in ancient times, and has since ceased to be so; all concur in demonstrating that the ground containing this ferment remains innocuous, as long as it is not placed in certain conditions indispensable to the multiplication of the specific ferment. Up to this point the parasitic organism lives, as it were, in a state of inertia, and may remain in that state for centuries, without losing any of its deleterious properties. Nor is this to be wondered at, for we know that the life and the power of evolution of the germs of beings, very superior to these minute ferment-producing organisms, can remain latent for centuries, and revive at once when they are placed in the conditions suitable for their development.

Amongst the conditions which favour the multiplication of the malarial ferment contained in the soil, and its successive accumulation in the superincumbent atmosphere, there are three absolutely essential, inasmuch as their concurrent action is indispensable to the production of malaria. These are—a temperature of not less than 20° Centigrade; a moderate degree of permanent humidity in the malarious soil; and lastly, a direct contact of the air with the strata of the earth which contain the ferment. If a single one of these three conditions be wanting, the development of malaria is rendered impossible. This is an important point in the natural history of malaria, because it gives us the key to most of the methods of sanitary improvement attempted by man.

Nature herself sometimes performs acts of sanitation in malarious lands, which suspend their morbific productions for a greater or less length of time. Winter, for instance, produces in all malarious countries a sanitation which is purely *thermic*; it suspends the production of malaria, simply because it causes a lowering of the temperature below the minimum necessary for its development. Indeed, if the temperature in winter rises above this minimum, there are often sudden outbreaks of malaria, even during that season. Again, during a very hot and dry summer, malaria does not develop itself, because the action of the sun's rays exhausts all the humidity in the soil, and thus produces a truly *hydraulic* sanitation, which may last a long time (as happened, for instance, in 1882, in the Agro Romano), but is easily put an end to by a single shower of rain. Nature may, moreover, furnish purely *atmospheric* sanitations, when the surface of the malarious soil is withdrawn from contact with the air, by means of a covering formed by a collection of water, or by the alluvial deposits of uninfected soil, or by means of a matting formed by the earth and the roots of the grasses growing closely together in a natural meadow.

Man imitates nature in his endeavours to impede the infectious productions of a malarious soil; that is to say, he seeks to eliminate at least one of the three conditions indispensable to the multiplication of the specific ferment contained in the soil. Naturally, he has never tried a *thermic* sanitation such as nature effects in winter, because it is not in his power to moderate the action of the sun. But it is in his power to accomplish atmospheric and hydraulic sanitations, and sometimes he has succeeded in combining both with success, by eliminating at the same time the humidity from the malarial soil and preventing its direct contact with the air.

Before proceeding to the study of the means which are proposed for effecting a permanent sanitation of the Agro Romano, let us first see what is the actual state of the production of malaria in that district and in Rome, and if there be any well-founded hope of impeding it, by means of hydraulic and atmospheric sanitation.

CHAPTER V.

THE AUTOCHTHONOUS PRODUCTION OF MALARIA IN THE TERRITORY OF ROME AND OF THE AGRO; AND THE SANITARY MEASURES PROPOSED FOR IMPEDING ITS DEVELOPMENT.

UNTIL within a few years, the question of the origin of Roman malaria, and of the measures to be adopted for the prevention of its development, was solved in theory without much difficulty. Some asserted that the Roman malaria came from the African swamps, and was brought over into the Roman district by the sirocco winds. To counteract that hypothetical importation, the only thing to be done, in their opinion, was to encourage the growth of woods and plantations along the sea-shore, as will be explained in the next chapter. The great majority, however, were satisfied with declaring that malaria came from the Pontine marshes and from the swamps of Ostia and Maccarese, through the agency of the sirocco; or even from the marshes of Stracciacappe and of Baccano, and from the lakes of the Tartari and of Pantano, by means of the winds which blow from other points of the compass. The hydraulic sanitation of those marshes, and of the few swampy spots marked on the hydrographical maps of that period, ought therefore to have sufficed to free Rome and its surrounding Agro from malaria. And, undoubtedly, if the malaria of Rome and of the adjacent districts had such an origin, the technical difficulties attending the sanitation of the Agro Romano and of the city would have been but small, compared with the immense benefit which would have been obtained.

But, unfortunately, such is not the case, and to satisfy ourselves on this point, we need only study the facts a little closely, making use of correctly drawn maps. In my investigations I have found that many of the errors, prevalent on this subject, have been caused by the incorrect setting of the maps of the province of Rome and of the Agro Romano. To economise space, and in order that the sea should not occupy too great a portion of the maps, these are so drawn as to have the sea across the bottom, close to the edge, and the chain of the Apennines across the top. And even when the arrow marking the north and south is depicted on those maps (and that does not always occur, even in the best guide-books and the best atlases), it is not easy to obtain a clear idea of the respective positions of the various portions of those regions, for it requires a great amount of reflection, in every instance, to arrange in one's mind the proper position of each place. Generally speaking, one receives the erroneous idea that the Pontine marshes are situated to the east of Rome, and that between them and the city there are no obstacles of any considerable height; and the mouths of the Tiber, together with the two swamps of Ostia and Maccarese, appear to lie to the south of Rome. Hence it seems possible, that the east and south winds might carry to Rome, the infected air of the Pontine marshes and of the swamps of Ostia and Maccarese. But when we study a map with proper bearings, the whole aspect of things is changed. To the south-east of Rome, rises up the great barrier of the Latial mountains, which separates the region of the Agro Romano from that of the Pontine marshes. No wind can possibly blow the malaria from the Pontine marshes towards Rome without encountering that obstacle. Even supposing for a moment that a wind could carry the malaria from such a great distance without dispersing it, we should be obliged, also, to believe that this malaria is carried up to the top of the Latial mountains, and then carried down to the Agro Romano,—an evident absurdity. We are therefore driven to abandon all idea of the importation of malaria from the Pontine marshes into the Agro Romano and Rome itself.

The swamps of Ostia and Maccarese do not lie to the south of Rome, as a cursory examination of the common maps would lead one to suppose. They lie to the southwest of Rome; no sirocco wind can possibly blow from them towards Rome, and the only wind which could possibly carry their malaria to Rome would be the libeccio (south-west). As yet no Roman doctor has discovered any relation between an outbreak of malarial fever and the blowing of the libeccio. Tacchini, on the contrary, has shown that, during the whole of the period between 1871–1882, the year, in which the libeccio blew most frequently during the most dangerous season, (that is, the third quarter of the year) was in 1882, which was the year during which there was the least amount of fever in the Roman region. And, in fact, if the libeccio were capable of carrying the malaria in a dangerous quantity from those two swamps to Rome, the three hills of Rome (the Quirinal, Viminal, and Esquiline), which are the most directly exposed to the action of that wind, ought to have been equally unhealthy at all times, and ought to continue to be so at the present day; whereas the Viminal was superior in healthiness to the Quirinal and the Esquiline, even when the greater portion of the soil of those three hills remained uncovered; and at the present time, when the two latter hills are covered over with houses and the pavement of streets, they also have become healthy, although, for certain, their position with respect to the two swamps has in no way changed.

Since the study of the natural history of malaria has progressed, the idea that it may be conveyed from great distances, in such a compact mass as to infect healthy atmospheres, is being gradually exploded: that idea, sprung from the marsh prejudice, which led people to ignore the malarious product taking place at their very feet, in numerous places that are not marshy and never were, is wrong. No one denies the fact that malaria can be conveyed to great distances by wind, for it would be absurd to do so. There is even reason for believing that the malarious germs, carried by winds to salubrious localities, and then precipitated by rain into the soil, have sometimes transformed it into malarious earth. But in such cases the fevers, which subsequently develop themselves in those localities, are to be ascribed to a malarious product which has become autochthonous in such places. Malaria is never conveyed in such a mass, as to produce infection directly amongst the inhabitants of a healthy district, unless for short distances and by atmospheric currents, moving at a rate inappreciable to any sense, except sight, when the poisonous air is laden with mist, and the eye can follow its extremely slow movement. Any aërial current of moderate velocity disperses the germs of malaria in such a manner, that it precludes the possibility of a dangerous malarious charging of the atmosphere of places which are at a distance from the hotbed of production. In Rome we have a most striking example of this during the hot season. The heat of Rome is more endurable than that of Florence, Milan, and Turin, because Rome enjoys a maritime climate, and, during the hottest hours of the day, the city is refreshed by a sea breeze. The breeze reaches Rome somewhat late, because Rome is several kilometres distant from the sea-shore—that is to say, about mid-day, and lasts till nearly sunset. It conveys fresh air from the sea, and penetrates the atmospherical strata, rarefied by the radiation of heat from the soil, throughout the whole extent of the Campagna which divides the sea from Rome, after having blown over all the swamps of the shore, and upon all the innumerable malarious hotbeds of the western portion of the Agro.

According to the theory of the conveyance of malaria from the marshes and swamps of the sea-shore to Rome, all its inhabitants ought to shut themselves up in their houses during the hours that this breeze blows; for at no other hour of the day could such conveyance be more direct or more marked. On the contrary, however, popular experience (which in questions of malaria is the best authority) proves quite the reverse, and every one enjoys with impunity the refreshing effect of this breeze, even in those years when malaria is most prevalent. It is not suggested that this breeze does not convey malaria to Rome. It does convey it thither, and even in considerable quantities; but whilst it brings malaria, it acts, at the same time, as a ventilator, by dispersing its germs in every direction. And if this gentle breeze disperses them in such a way as to render them quite innocuous, how great must be the dispersion of the malaria of Ostia, of Maccarese, and, generally speaking, of the Tibertine delta, if carried to Rome by an atmospheric current so swift and so impetuous as that of the libeccio?

The same thing may be said of the malaria generated in the marshes of Stracciacappe and of Baccano, and in the lakes of the Tartari, and of Pantano. During the evenings of summer and of early autumn, a couple of hours after sunset, the population of Rome pours forth into the streets and the piazzas to enjoy the refreshing effects of another breeze. People seat themselves placidly in the Piazza

Colonna, or elsewhere, where music is played in the open air, and have no fear of remaining exposed to that breeze. That evening breeze, what is it? It is no other than the land breeze, common to all maritime countries, created by the movement towards the sea of the atmospherical strata that cover the soil, which have cooled a great deal earlier than the atmospherical strata that cover the surface of the sea. That aërial current draws towards Rome the exhalations of that portion of the Agro which divides Rome from the mountains; but, as usual, whilst drawing them thither it acts as a ventilator, and not only disperses them, so as to render them harmless, but disperses also in like manner the exhalations of a similar nature accumulated in Rome after sunset. In fact, in some parts of the city the inhabitants, during the hot weather, remain indoors after sunset, because experience has taught them that during the first hour of the evening there is a risk of infection; but later on they emerge from their houses (at the very time when that breeze from the surrounding Campagna passes over Rome), because experience has also taught them that there is no danger then to be apprehended. And if so weak a current of air can produce such a dispersion of the malaria, how much more complete must be the dispersion caused by winds capable of carrying directly to Rome the exhalations of the distant marshes of Stracciacappe, and of Baccano, and of the lakes of the Tartari and of Pantano?

That the best possible methods should be adopted for the sanitation of all those marshes is most desirable; and the reasons for this are so obvious that there is no necessity to enumerate them. But it cannot be admitted that the sanitation of those marshes can, in any appreciable manner, modify the hygienic conditions of Rome and of the greater portion of the Agro. It would improve, if properly carried out, the hygienic conditions of the places where those marshes are situated, and their immediate neighbourhood. But how could it possibly have any effect upon the much more extensive production of malaria which occurs throughout the whole of the Agro Romano, and in a portion, not inconsiderable even at the present day, of Rome itself? In Rome malaria is produced in many spots where the soil is still uncovered, or where the labour of man places it in direct contact with the air; and certainly it is not by the extinction of distant marsh-malarious hotbeds, that any important amelioration of the situation will be arrived at.

The vast complications of the problem respecting the sanitation of the Agro Romano become the more evident, the more closely the question is studied. The history of this country is of itself sufficient to show how difficult the endeavour must be. If the strenuous labours of such agriculturists and practical hydraulic engineers as the Etruscans, the Latins, the Volscians, and the Romans—if the accumulated work of centuries on the Roman territory, did not succeed in freeing it from that pestilence, except after a great lapse of time, and never in a perfect manner, it is evident that the question to be dealt with is one of no ordinary difficulty. It cannot be said that we are superior to the ancients in our knowledge of the subject; and it may be that, from a practical point of view, we are inferior; as everything seems to prove that their intellects were not clouded by the marsh prejudice, which we have only been able to shake off quite lately. If we have the advantage over them, from a scientific point of view, of having demonstrated that malaria is a living ferment, and of having determined satisfactorily the conditions which render its multiplication difficult, we are still very far from knowing how to render its existence impossible, where the earth must preserve the qualities of a vegetable soil. And when, as is the case with the Roman Cam-

G

pagna, we have to deal with soils which, however variable they may be, as regards site, geological composition, and hydrographical conditions, show themselves capable of producing malaria, it behoves us to be very modest in our assertions and our promises.

As to that part of the region which is occupied by the city of Rome, the solution of the problem has been facilitated by the progressive increase of the population therein since 1870. When the capital of Italy was transferred to Rome, matters stood as shown by the malaria map of the city, which I drew up in accordance with very accurate data, furnished by two distinguished Roman Doctors, Lanzi and Terrigi. At first sight, that map gives an impression that the portions of the city situated in the plain are healthy, and the hills malarious; and thus one might conclude that the opinion, till then prevalent, was fully borne out—that is; that these latter were unhealthy, because the malaria-bearing winds, blowing from the distant marshes, strike the hills in a more direct manner than they do the lower parts of the city. But upon a closer examination, we find that such is not the case. With the exception of the Viminal, all those parts of the town, where the soil was still uncovered, were unhealthy, and, where they were covered by the pavement of the streets and by the houses built on them, irrespective of plain or hill, they were healthy.

The exception of the Viminal is strange, as at that time it was almost entirely uncovered, and yet was considered as healthy by all the inhabitants living on it. Whether this salubrity of the Viminal was due to the great distance which separated the surface of its soil from the level of its subterranean waters, or to other causes, I cannot undertake to say. I can only assert it as a fact, and so well-established a fact, that it was put forward by myself and others as an argument when the question of building the new quarters on the hills was being discussed. All the interests concerned in concentrating the development of Rome on the low-lying parts of the city were urgent in maintaining that all the hills of Rome were malarious, and were malarious in a perfectly incurable way, inasmuch as malaria was brought to them from the marshes of the Agro, and especially from those on the seashore.

We opposed to this view the fact of the salubrity of the Viminal, which is situated between the Esquiline and the Quirinal, for if the malaria of these last two hills were imported, instead of being autochthonous, the former would of necessity have been equally infected. We said: —"The Viminal is salubrious, in spite of its uncovered soil, because this soil is not malarious; the Esquiline and Quirinal are unhealthy, because their uncovered soil produces malaria. And, therefore, it is most probable that they also will become salubrious if such a development of building operations should take place as would prevent the direct contact of their malarious soil with the overhanging atmosphere over an extensive area."

And this is precisely what did occur, and not only in the case of the Esquiline and the Quirinal. If a comparison be made between the malaria map of 1870, which I have been referring to, and the malaria map of 1884, drawn up likewise, principally from statistics collected with great care by Doctors Lanzi and Terrigi, it will be seen how many portions of Rome, which were malarious in 1870, have since become salubrious. They remained malarious as long as the soil lay exposed, but ceased so to be when, between the soil and the atmosphere, a sort of impermeable coat of varnish was interposed, in the shape of the pavement of the streets and the erection of new buildings.

This is one of the modes of sanitation which I call *atmospheric*, because they are constituted by a simple cessation of direct contact between the malarious soil and the atmosphere; and it is a means which keeps increasing in proportion with the increase of the population of the city.

It would also appear to be proved that an atmospheric sanitation may be obtained without covering the ground with buildings, especially should such be combined with hydraulic improvements. In fact, in the old botanical garden of the Lungara, which was a particularly malarious spot, a successful sanitation has been obtained by putting the drainage of the gardens into proper order, by thinning out the trees, and by transforming into thickly-sown meadows, all those portions of the land which are not covered by the macadam of the avenues and of the parade ground attached to the new Military College. This College was installed in the Salviati Palace, after the improvements in the old botanical garden had been completed, and, until now, no case of malarial fever has occurred amongst the large number of persons who live there.

But, for all this, we must not suppose that this kind of sanitation has extinguished the malaria, which is contained in the soil of the city. It has rendered its pestilential manifestation impossible, by suppressing one of the conditions essential to its development—that is, the immediate contact of the infected earth with the air. But if that contact be accidentally restored in any way, as, for example, by an excavation made in hot weather, and when the soil is damp, the three conditions necessary for the multiplication of the malarious ferment become once more re-established, and we have the unpleasant surprise of experiencing an outbreak of malaria in places which had previously been rendered salubrious. Notwithstanding this, however, those atmospheric sanitations, provided they be continually kept up, are amongst the most efficacious; and by their means the city of Rome will become free of malaria throughout all those parts which do not immediately adjoin the surrounding Campagna. The great benefits already realized are a good reason for entertaining this confidence, bearing in mind, moreover, that those benefits accrued independently of any hydraulic improvements made in the Agro; for in reality, until 1884 none had been made. The remarkable sanitation already produced in Rome between 1870 and 1884 is due to the gradual keeping down of the autochthonous malaria of the city, and to no other cause.

It is not possible to form an opinion on the actual malarious production, in the different portions of the Agro, with the same accuracy as we can, in the various districts of Rome. We know that throughout the whole extent of the Agro, malaria prevails; but whether there be some exceptionally healthy spots, such as the Viminal was before 1870 in Rome, it is impossible to determine with any certainty. It is possible to draw up a malaria map of Rome, because in Rome, everywhere, we have, in a greater or less quantity, a reagent which reveals positively the existence of the obnoxious product, and enables us to appreciate its intensity. And this reagent is *man*, with a fixed residence during the whole year. But as to the drawing up of a malaria map of the Agro, that is impossible as yet. Immense tracts of land possess no habitations whatever; and the great majority of the persons, who inhabit the Agro during spring and winter, migrate in the summer, and do not return until late in the autumn.

Under such circumstances any attempt to arrive at a correct conclusion, respecting the differences in the malarious production of the Agro Romano, is bound to fail. The human reagent (the only sure test of the existence of malaria in a locality) is a scarce article there, or is absent altogether during the fever season; and the information obtained by questioning the people of the Campagna cannot be relied upon. In addition to the erroneous statements made in all good faith (and they are not a few), there is a risk of collecting a great many others which are not made in good faith at all. Sometimes they imagine that you are a collector of taxes, and tell you that the place is pestiferous, although it is not; in order that you may not be induced to raise their assessment. At other times they take you for a would-be purchaser, and assert that the place is healthy, even when it is extremely malarious, in order to induce you to buy. Cases are known in which they will tell you a falsehood rather than speak the truth, for fear of ruining their trade. A person not long ago asked a publican, in the neighbourhood of Rome, whether there was any malaria at his place. It is a spot which may safely be frequented in winter and spring, and with comfort, for there is a good tavern, and consequently it is greatly patronized, but in summer the place is very dangerous. The host perceived from the accent of his interlocutor that he was not a Roman, and knowing that strangers are greatly afraid of Roman fever, even in winter, and not wishing to have the reputation of his tavern jeopardized, he replied that it was a most delightful locality even in summer. How could a map be drawn up from such information? We must admit that malaria prevails throughout the whole extent of the Campagna, although there are abundant reasons for believing that some localities are much more malarious than others, and that some are entirely free from it. But in the present state of things, it is not possible to make any positive statement, nor can any sure indication be drawn from the position or the hydrographical condition of places. In the Agro Romano, there are places on the hills which are much more malarious than some on the plains, and also grounds resting on lava, and with excellent natural drainage, which give out a great deal of malaria. Around Rome there are well-cultivated vineyards, in which the hydrographical and topographical conditions of the soil appear to be excellent, and which are quite as unhealthy as some of the most deserted lands of the Agro Romano. If even in the course of time a perfect hydraulic improvement of the Agro should be achieved, (a thing not so easy as is generally supposed), we could not guarantee the suspension of the malarious production of that region. There is a hydraulic factor which is beyond the control of man, that is, rain, which of itself is sufficient to neutralize the effect of a hydraulic sanitation. This is proved by the fact, that in many spots in the Agro, no fever shows itself when the spring is deficient in rain and the summer is very hot and dry. Whereas, if during the existence of that hydraulic sanitation produced by nature, should a heavy downfall of rain occur, an unexpected outbreak of malaria ensues. For this reason it would be desirable to add an atmospheric sanitation to the hydraulic one of the Agro, in order to make the effects of the latter more certain.

But how is this to be accomplished? With the exception of well-kept meadows, we know of no other form of cultivation, which is of any value in reducing the direct contact of the atmosphere with the malarious soil; on the contrary, all other forms of cultivation produce a diametrically opposite effect, owing to the necessary turning up of the soil, which increases the surface of immediate contact. To cover over the malarious soil with layers of uninfected earth is, humanly speaking, impossible, as regards the hills of the Agro; and as to the valleys, although in theory the thing might be done, in practice it is not feasible. To transport thither by hand, earth taken from salubrious places would be a work of such colossal proportions as to render the attempt a folly. To cause the streams which run through the valleys, to deposit their mould on the surface of the latter, might be possible—but what would be the nature of this mould? The sediment which all these streams, with the exception of the Tiber and the Arno, carry along, is composed entirely of the earth of the Agro Romano itself, and consequently is malarious. It would be only adding more soil of the same nature to the Roman valleys, which are already filled, and over-filled, with malarious earth which has descended from the hills of the Agro.

The mould carried by the Tiber could supply some of the lower-lying localities of its great valley with earth fillings, salubrious as well as productive. That the Tiber does carry along productive soil is a fact so well known as not to require demonstration; and that it is generally of a salubrious nature, is a statement which can be verified throughout the course of that river, and in Rome itself. In Tuscany and elsewhere, fillings from the mould of the Tiber have been made, which are productive and in nowise malarious; and in Rome, along the S. Spirito hospital, there is a bank of earth thrown up by the Tiber, which has been turned during many years, into a kitchen garden, and never did give out malaria. In fact, not only myself with my temporary pathological institute, but many others before me, have been located many years near that bank, whilst it was a kitchen garden, and no one ever suffered. It is greatly to be desired that, in the sanitation of the valley of the Tiber, its deposits should be utilized to fill up the hollows instead of allowing them to be carried out uselessly into the sea, where their only effect is to prolong indefinitely the delta of the river.

A good opportunity of making a Tibertine filling, useful both to agriculture and to health, was offered by the sanitation of the swamps of Ostia and Maccarese decreed by the law of 1878. Father Secchi and Marchese Raffaele Pareto, knowing the extreme uncertainty of the sanitation of malarial basins by means of the simple drawing off of the waters which are accumulated in them, had proposed to convert those two swamps into permanent lakes, as was done with the marsh of Averno—that is, to fill them up with water. That plan, however, had to be abandoned on account of the enormous cost of deepening those two vast basins, and of raising the banks so as to allow of the water let in being always kept at an uniform level. One other plan remained, which was to fill them up with the deposits of the Tiber, which is the best of filling-rivers, as the Tiber, even in its smallest floods, always brings down an immense quantity of earth. But with the preconceived notion, that the unhealthiness of the city of Rome was due, chiefly to the exhalations from those two swamps, it was thought necessary to suppress these at once; and, always with the idea that malaria comes from stagnant waters, and not from the soil on which they stagnate, the plan of the Tibertine-filling process was rejected, and a design was accepted of obtaining an agricultural and hygienic amelioration of that zone, by persistently drawing off the waters of the two swamps by means of hydrovorous machines, and so transforming them into two *polders*.

Whether, from an agricultural point of view, it was a happy idea to abandon the improvement of the soil of those two swamps by filling them up, once for all, with productive earth, and to lay bare instead their bottom (which, besides being impregnated with salt water, is mostly sandy and slimy), charging the property, moreover, with a perpetual yearly expenditure for the maintenance of the hydrovorous machines, is a matter which it is not my business to inquire into. From a hygienic point of view it was a most unfortunate decision. The Tibertine-filling guaranteed a diminution in the malaria production of those basins, and afforded substantial ground for hoping to succeed in checking it. The mechanical desiccation will at first have the effect of increasing it, laying bare those parts of the bottom of the two swamps, which even in summer remain covered over by a sheet of water. And no one can foretell whether this increase of the malaria production will not last, even after the work of desiccation is completed.

The transformation of lakes, swamps, and generally of marshy places into *polders*, that is to say, into basins kept dry by means of hydrovorous machines, is a hydraulic-agricultural operation peculiar to the Low Countries. Immense tracts of land there, have been reclaimed from the sea and devoted to agriculture by means of that system, making use of hydrovorous machines, driven by windmills in the past, and by steam in the present day. The inhabitants of those countries have no other way of converting the lowlands submerged by water into arable ground, for they cannot get natural fillings of mould from the rivers which flow through their territories, and it would be madness to attempt to fill up such vast and deep depressions with imported earth. For centuries past, the reclamation of land from the sea has gone on increasing and improving in Holland, giving rise to an agricultural industry which is a model of its kind. But even in those northern latitudes the operation is not free from danger; because, although the most malarious of those lands are not to be compared, as to their infectious power, with the malarious lands of Central and Southern Italy, still, it very often happens that when the waters which cover the soil are removed, the earth gives forth malaria in abundance.

Very serious malarious epidemics often break out after the mechanical desiccation, as happened, for example, in 1857, when the lake of Haarlem was transformed into a polder of 18,000 hectares in extent. In many places that development of malaria in the polders has become permanent. Nor are the polder fevers of the Low Countries of no importance. It is seldom that in those regions they assume the violent form of our deadly fevers; but they are often very obstinate, and capable of ruining a man's constitution for life, in the same way as the chronic malarious infection of our climate. In order to obviate those consequences as much as possible, it has been decided, in Holland, to increase the power of the hydrovorous machines, so that the level of the subterranean waters of the polders may be kept at a very low point. In the polder of the Y, (an arm of the sea near Amsterdam which was desiccated in 1873—78), machines were employed of sufficient power to maintain the level of those waters, at a metre below the level of the soil already dried up and solidified; and as late as last year there had been no outbreak of fever in that region. It remains to be proved whether that immunity in the Y is not due to the absence of malarious ferment in the soil of the locality, rather than to the beneficial results derived from the use of hydraulic works, because along the coasts in the North, it is not an uncommon thing to see basins situated at short distances from one another, in some of which malaria develops itself, and in others it does not, although they possess the same climatic conditions, and, apparently, the same geological and hydrographical conditions. It can only be after the new system shall have been applied to a considerable number of other polders in Holland, both old and new, that that doubt can be settled, and that it can be affirmed that it is capable of guaranteeing the salubrity obtained by means of hydraulic operations.

But, granted that that is proved, so far as the polders of Holland are concerned, and granted also that it is possible and practicable to apply the system, adopted in the Y, to the polders of Ostia and Maccarese, who can be sure that it will prevent the development of malaria there? The malaria charge of the Roman soil, especially in that region, is much greater than that of the soil of Holland and of Belgium; and we know by painful experience how small a quantity of humidity is sufficient to call into active operation the noxious productions of that soil. I have already pointed out that it not infrequently happens, that when the spring rains have been scarce, and the summer very dry and hot, the production of malaria in the Agro Romano remains in abeyance; but a single shower is sufficient at times to restore its intensity, so as to fill the hospitals of Rome with fever-stricken patients. In the plan adopted for the polders of Ostia and Maccarese, the water in the network of the canals of those polders, will rise to a much higher point than a metre below the level of the desiccated and compact lands, which is the point reached by the water in all the canals of the Y. In consequence, the dampness of the soil of our polders will be ever so much greater than that of those polders in Holland, which, until now, are the only ones which have not proved themselves detrimental to the public health.

For all those reasons I proposed in 1885 to the Minister of Public Works, to complete the canalization of all the upper waters on the seaboard of the Agro Romano, but not to undertake to deal with the lower waters, until a fresh and exhaustive examination should have been made, of the advisability of filling up the two swamps with Tibertine mould. I made the proposal simply as a matter of conscience, from the firm conviction which I entertained, of the mistake which was about to be committed, and not with the expectation of its being attended to. There were too many interests and too many personal vanities mixed up in this matter, and my request was refused. Now, without being a prophet, it is easy to foretell that matters will proceed in this wise—the mechanical desiccation will be carried out, and then, later on, when its imperfections are recognized, the Tibertine filling will be adopted. The ultimate result, whenever it takes place, will be the same; but it will have been obtained by a double process and at a double expense.

In order to facilitate the hydraulic sanitation of some parts of the Agro, a sort of superficial drainage has been devised, by means of plantations capable of sucking up a great quantity of the water from the soil. With the preconceived idea that malaria is caused by the putrid decompositions of marshy lands, it was suggested that an attempt should be made in that direction with eucalyptus trees. It was thought that those trees, which are of very rapid growth, would dry up the swampy lands, and at the same time, destroy the miasmatic exhalations with the aroma of their leaves. Until now, there is no record, as far as I know, of a case of sanitation brought about by means of eucalyptus only; but I would not, for that reason, deny the possibility of such a result. There is nothing to preclude the admission that such plantations have sometimes proved to be of great use in certain malarious lands. I maintain, however, that in many instances they have not been of any service; and it is well to guard one's self against exaggerations on that subject, as they often warp the judgment. Such exaggerations might have been avoided, and the consequent disappointment as well, if, instead of talking of those plantations as a question of theory, the first step had been taken, of studying the effects of the eucalyptus in its native country; and then it would have been ascertained in time that, even in the Australian hemisphere, where the eucalyptus flourishes a great deal better than with us, there are groves of eucalyptus trees where the development of malaria is very extensive, according to the statement of Professor Liversidge, of the University of Sydney, in Australia. Even in Italy, where everybody was convinced from the newspaper reports that the farm of the

Tre Fontane, near Rome, had become salubrious by means of plantations of eucalyptus, we had the very unpleasant surprise of an unexpected outbreak of malaria there in 1882, which attacked the *whole* of that agricultural colony; whereas, throughout the rest of the Roman Campagna, an unusual amount of salubrity prevailed. The surprise would not have been so great, if the public had been aware of the exertions that were made to hide the vicissitudes which that colony underwent immediately after its foundation in 1880; and as these facts are very instructive, I may be permitted to narrate them here.

To the left of the Via Ostiense, and at a distance of five kilometres from Rome, is situated the Abbey of the Tre Fontane. In that abbey there is a monastery of Trappists, who for many years had striven to improve the agricultural condition of the land in the neighbourhood of the monastery, by means of extensive plantations of vines, by a system of drainage of the soil, and by planting eucalyptus trees. It was said that, concurrently with the agricultural improvement obtained by those means, a hygienic amelioration had also been achieved, and that the intensity of the malaria, which the place produced, had been reduced. That benefit was, by the public generally, and likewise by the government officials, attributed to the eucalyptus plantations, and to the use of a eucalyptus liqueur manufactured by the Trappists; and in consequence the idea of extending that particular cultivation was suggested. Adjacent to the Tre Fontane there was a farm of 495 hectares, formerly belonging to the Sisters of the Holy Sacrament, for the lease of which a bid had been made by an association of fifty families of peasants, who intended to establish there an inhabited centre, in accordance with the terms of the law concerning the sanitation of the Agro Romano. But the administrators of the ecclesiastical domains refused to enter into negotiations with those free agriculturists, and let this estate to the Trappists, with the object of undertaking an extensive sanitation by means of eucalyptus plantations.

In order to assist that experiment, in 1880 a penal colony of convicts was established at the Tre Fontane, and housed in barracks close to the monastery, and in that portion of the old farm which was commonly believed to have already been benefited by the eucalyptus trees. The hygienic conditions of those convicts (as to their hours of work, lodgings, food, and clothing) were far superior to those which the agriculturists of the Campagna of Rome possess. Notwithstanding all those advantages, scarcely had the fever season of 1880 set in, than all the members of the penal colony began to suffer from malarious infection, in a more or less severe form. The conviction, which had now become well rooted in the public mind, that at the Tre Fontane any one might live without risk during the fever season (thanks to the eucalyptus trees and the eucalyptus liqueur), had led the founders of the colony to neglect many precautions, and the consequence was, that the loss of many lives had to be deplored, even amongst the convict guards. At first the fact was denied; then, when there was no possibility of concealing it, an attempt was made to explain it away by saying that inasmuch as that year the malaria had broken out in great force throughout the Campagna of Rome, the atmosphere of the Tre Fontane had become unusually infected by the admixture of the mephitic air of the surrounding localities. However, in 1881 it was thought advisable to take greater precautions, and when in 1882 the colonizing experiment was repeated on a larger scale, every desirable precaution was taken in good time, in order that immediate assistance might be rendered to any one who unfortunately should be attacked by malaria.

During the summer and autumn of 1882, *all the*

inhabitants of the Tre Fontane were attacked. The Trappists, it would appear, had the fever only slightly, but still they all had it. Some of the convicts had mild attacks, but others severe and dangerous ones, and, after they were cured, it was necessary to send them to the prisons of Civita Vecchia and Spoleto to recruit their health. Almost all the convict guards had violent attacks of fever, and had to be sent away. There were no deaths; but this was due to assistance being at hand, and rendered by active and able doctors, who placed their patients in the infirmary of Regina Cœli, which had been expressly enlarged, and who succeeded by specific remedies, (three kilogrammes of quinine were consumed) and powerful tonics, to save the colony. But long after the cure of the feverish attacks, the proofs of their severity were evident in the impoverished state of the blood of many of the convicts, and of almost the whole of the convict guards.

Those facts led the medical men of the colony of Tre Fontane to suggest, that in the ensuing year the works should be discontinued during the most dangerous months. And I also, in the House of Deputies, on January 22nd, 1883, repeated that suggestion to the Minister of the Interior, moved thereto principally by the sad state to which the convict guards had been reduced by the fever. These, in fact, were always more severely attacked than the convicts, both in 1880 and in 1882. Perhaps the want of movement, which their duty of watching during the long hours of the convicts' work entailed upon them, may have been the cause of retaining within their system, a large amount of the malarious ferment inhaled with the air they breathed; whereas the convicts' systems were able to throw off a considerable quantity of it, in consequence of their greater amount of bodily exertions and of the abundance of some of the secretions induced thereby. However it might be, it did not appear to me right that those guards should be exposed to the danger of catching such a serious complaint in the discharge of a service which was not a State duty. In fact, many circumstances which it would be out of place to enumerate here, deprived the works at the Tre Fontane of the character of an agricultural experiment undertaken for the public good, and gave them the character of a private speculation carried on for the benefit of the Trappists and their associates.

But I addressed myself to deaf men; I only succeeded in wounding many susceptibilities and offending many interests engaged in that undertaking, and obtained no practical result, save that the medical men of the colony were removed, and others appointed in their stead. Everything was denied. In similar cases that is the best way of getting out of a scrape. The Minister of the Interior presented to the Chamber a return, showing the average of hospital cases from the colony for twenty-four months, to prove how few they were, and I do not wish to doubt the correctness of that return. Its only defect was that it related to a different period to the one in which the attacks occurred. As for myself, I cannot tell the insults levelled at me for having dared to expose those facts, especially on the part of the French press; for all the Trappists of the Tre Fontane were Frenchmen, with the exception of the abbot. With many persons the question of deciding whether malaria existed or not at the Tre Fontane, became a matter of supporting the views of a Deputy of the kingdom of Italy, or of an united body of French ecclesiastics. I was invited to a controversy by some; but from what I have already said, it is easy to guess that I remained more than ever true to my determination of not entering into any controversy on the subject of malaria. Controversy in such a matter is always useless, and oftentimes it is detrimental to the cause of science; for we have always to contend with too many interests which are in no wise scientific. The great point is never to assert anything which is not certain, and to leave the remainder to time, which in the end brings to light the truth of facts, should they be correct. And so it really did happen in the question of the Tre Fontane. After the penal colony had experienced some other severe malarial attacks, especially in the year 1885, everybody felt that the farce was played out. The Government stopped the so-called experiment, and took back the convicts; the Italian abbot, who had assumed the part of leaseholder, disappeared; and the only practical result of the whole operation was this: the big estate of which an Italian sisterhood had been dispossessed by the secularisation of the Italian monasteries, belongs now to a French brotherhood that had hidden itself behind the Italian leaseholder. By our Italian laws this lease is perpetual. That result explains all the facts which I have stated, and gives us, once more, an example of what may be done by persons who know how to make a clever use of a hygienic pretence.

If to the many most reasonable doubts regarding the hygienic effects which are to be derived from eucalyptus trees, there be added the uncertain economical results to be procured from a plantation of them, it must be conceded that the enthusiasm respecting the eucalyptus is quite unjustified. Those trees, in fact, are very capricious. As they are in full sap during the winter of our hemisphere, they are often killed by a wintry frost, by cold humidity, by the late frosts of the spring, and by other causes which as yet botanists have failed to discover. At other times, in places where the winter is mild, and the soil of great depth, those trees increase in height too rapidly, and are snapped off like reeds by moderate winds. Besides, it must be remembered that a plantation of those trees often entails a heavy cost. If the soil happens to be swampy it must be drained, otherwise the roots of the eucalyptus become rotten. If, on the other hand, the soil is hard, it must be dug to a great depth, and furrows made to receive the straggling roots of those trees, which often require to be drained off, in order to prevent the permeating waters stagnating in them and causing the roots to rot. It is better therefore to confine ourselves to methods of hydraulic sanitation which are less uncertain; and whenever the nature of the soil suggests the experiment of planting trees possessing strongly absorbent qualities, it is better to choose trees of our own hemisphere. Less money will be spent, and they will not die so easily.

It is often said in Rome that the plantations at the Tre Fontane have increased the salubrity of that city by filtering the malaria of the sea-shore swamps wafted by winds towards the city. Were such the case the improvement would naturally be most noticeable in the southern portion of Rome, which is the nearest to the Tre Fontane. But it is precisely in that southern part of the city that there has been no appreciable improvement in the atmosphere since 1870, for the very good reason that building operations have not been extended in that direction, so as to keep under, the noxious exhalations of the soil. Let it not be supposed that I have called attention to this fantastical notion which is current in Rome, for the purpose of discussing it. I have done so, simply with the object of giving a ready example of the strange application made of an erroneous theory, which will be the subject of the next chapter.

CHAPTER VI.

FORESTS AND THE ROMAN MALARIA.

AMONGST the prejudices which prevail in different parts of the world respecting malaria, one of the most widely-spread is the notion which attributes to forests the property of generating it spontaneously; that is to say, independently of the quality of the soil on which these stand. That prejudice is based upon facts which may be verified in every portion of the globe situated between the two Polar circles. Everywhere forests are to be met with in which malaria abounds, and everywhere are to be found vast tracts of country which were uninhabitable as long as they remained forests, and which have become more or less salubrious after they have been deforested.

Most persons account for those facts by supposing that malaria develops itself by means of the putrefaction of leaves, of branches, and of dead insects, which accumulate on the ground and there undergo a slow process of decomposition. But such an explanation will not hold good, because, were such the case, malaria ought to exist in every forest throughout the world in which this putrid decomposition of organic detritus takes place; whereas there are many forests which are quite free from malaria, although the quantity of vegetable and animal detritus which are there accumulated, and putrify, is enormous. For the same reason another explanation is also inadmissible: that forests generate fevers because people enter into them coming from sunny places and therefore get chilled. There are forests that are remarkably cool, even in summer, and in which no one has ever caught a fever; whereas other forests lying in plains from which all ventilation is excluded, and in which the temperature is often higher than in the surrounding open country, are extremely malarious.

Forests do not generate malaria except indirectly; they do not produce it spontaneously, but encourage its development when the ground upon which they stand is of a malarious nature. They intercept the rays of the sun, and thereby prevent the active evaporation of the soil, so that a great amount of humidity is retained during the hot weather, even in those strata which are in direct contact with the atmosphere. If those superficial strata of the soil do not contain the malarial ferment the forest is harmless, but should that ferment exist in those strata, then the forest favours the production of malaria, because it preserves them in a state of humidity. And inasmuch as, unfortunately, that particular infection of the soil is spread widely throughout nature, the instances of malarious forests occur very frequently, and as frequently occur instances of hygienic amelioration by a process of deforesting. When we remove from land in this infected condition the obstacle which hindered the direct action of the rays of the sun upon it, its desiccation by the heat of summer diminishes its malarial productiveness, and even arrests it sometimes under favourable circumstances.

Although an experience so generally disseminated has recognized that fact, and has made use of it to reclaim from malaria, vast tracts of cultivable soil both in the Old and the New worlds; in Rome, on the contrary, the belief prevails, that in a malarious country woods ought not only to be preserved, but their number increased. Ignorant people talk of sirocco winds which carry malaria to Rome from the real or imaginary swamps of Africa, and of the consequent necessity of offering to those winds a barrier of shore-forests, which may retain in their leaves the morbific effluvia of foreign origin. They do not consider that, if such were the cause of the Roman malaria, Marsala, which is the city of Italy most directly exposed to the current of the true African sirocco, ought to be pestilential, instead of being the salubrious town which it is ; and that on all occasions when the sirocco blows, people navigating on the southern parts of the Mediterranean ought to catch the fever, a fact which has never occurred, nor is likely ever to occur.

Educated persons talk of the malaria produced by the marshes on the Roman littoral which the sirocco winds carry into Rome, and therefore think that it is well to have between Rome and those seashore marshes, a system of natural filters such as forests would offer. But inasmuch as it is well known how malaria is produced throughout the whole, or nearly the whole, region of the Agro Romano, and that strong winds disperse it instead of carrying it along in pestiferous quantities, it seems almost a waste of time to discuss such a theory. Still, after all, it may not be entirely useless, because the idea has taken root in Rome ever since the commencement of the last century, and to many persons, even at the present day, it would appear a matter of high treason to cast any doubt upon it, out of deference to its distinguished inventor, Lancisi.

For that reason, therefore, it may not be amiss to investigate the question. And this advantage may be derived from its study : that it will afford an instance of the strange aberrations into which a strong mind may be led, when it allows itself to deal with natural history, without a minute and exhaustive study of facts and places, and by working at a desk from imaginary data.

In 1714 Michael Angelo Caetani, Duke of Sermoneta, contracted with a merchant of Leghorn to cut down some of his forests in the Pontine marshes, and especially a wood situated to the south of Cisterna, between that town and the marshes. Difficulties arose, it is not known of what nature, probably on the part of the inhabitants of Cisterna, who were about to lose the freedom of pasture and the privilege of cutting wood in that forest. Pope Clement XI. wished to have the case decided by a Commission appointed for the purpose, before which Giovanni Maria Lancisi, a famous physician of the time, was called as an expert. He set forth his views in two discourses delivered in Latin, according to the custom of the day, and published by him in Latin as an appendix to his work, *De Noxiis Paludum Effluviis*. Those discourses were originally written in Italian, and the Italian text is still preserved in the Lancisiana Library at the Hospital of St. Spirito in Rome. And it is well that they have been preserved, for we are thereby enabled to form a more correct notion of Lancisi's real views, which, expressed by himself in a living language, are not enveloped in the vague and indeterminate forms to which one is generally obliged to have recourse, when discussing questions relating to modern life, in Latin.

Lancisi undertook the performance of his task, as an expert, without visiting the spot, which he had never seen. He admits it himself, and says that he was satisfied with studying a map of the forests in question, and reading a description of them. As a result of that study, however, he does not seem to have conceived a correct notion of their true topographical position; for, from the very outset, he attributes to those forests an influence on the general salubrity of Rome. Evidently he believed in the malaria being carried from the Pontine marshes to Rome, and that of itself is sufficient to show that he consulted very erroneous maps, or that he was not able to understand their proper bearings.

Lancisi's starting point was that malaria is only produced in marshy localities, and believed that non-marshy places affected by malaria might be freed from it, if between them and the marshy regions, barriers were interposed capable of intercepting it. Lancisi had taken into his head that the best barrier against malaria was one composed of woods, because the leaves of the trees retained it, acting as a filter; and, moreover, he was of opinion that this forest filter was a barrier much more efficacious than any other intercepting obstacle, *even should this be a hill higher than the top of the plantations.* And in support of that theory of his, he put forward two sorts of arguments—historical and scientific.

I shall not enter into any long examination of the historical arguments put forth by Lancisi, as otherwise I should find myself in an inextricable maze, considering the quantity of extraneous rubbish dug out of ancient authors which he imports into the case. I will only deal with his principal argument, which he deduces from the sacred character of many of the groves of antiquity. Inasmuch as some of those sacred groves were dedicated to Æsculapius, the tutelary divinity of medicine, he infers without any further proof that, without doubt, those groves had the effect of protecting the health of human beings. But he overlooked the fact, that a few only of such groves were dedicated to Æsculapius, and that by far the greater number were dedicated to divinities of a nature the reverse of beneficent.

All the primitive temples of the nations of antiquity, and especially of Greece and Italy, to whatever divinity dedicated, were composed of an altar set up in the open air, in some spot bounded by a hedge, by a palisade, or by a bank of earth, in which there was a plantation of greater or less extent. The wood was the temple. The obscurity of forests, and the long periods of silence, broken at intervals by the confused noises heard in them, have ever suggested, from the first dawn of civilization, the idea that woods were mysterious retreats, inhabited by good or evil spirits. Primitive religions availed themselves of this idea, transforming those spirits into positive myths, and consecrating to them the woods in which they had their abode: that is to say, in other words, by proclaiming that a specified wood was the exclusive property of the supernatural being whose presence therein was recognized, and declaring it to be the permanent residence of such being.

The conservative tendencies natural to all religions, perpetuated this primordial idea, and when the advance of civilization procured for the divinity a more worthy abode, by erecting a walled temple around the altar, what remained of the primitive temple, the wood, still retained its sacred character.

Neither the question of health, nor Æsculapius, had anything to do with the matter; for we find the most sacred groves of antiquity generally dedicated to the most cruel and truculent divinities. And it is only natural that it should be so, for ever since the world has been a world, people have always paid more respect to those who have it in their power to do them harm, than to those who may do, or have done, them good. In Western Europe the most venerated groves were those in Auvergne, dedicated to the god Esus, to whom the Druids offered up entire hecatombs of human victims, and those near Genzano, dedicated to *Diana Nemorensis*, to whom, without doubt, in ancient times human sacrifices were offered, for even in very civilized days the tradition was kept up by the fact, that the office of high priest of the goddess was obtained by slaying the actual holder of the office.

And inasmuch as human sacrifices were not offered to beneficent divinities, who viewed them with horror, but to evil divinities, that they might provide those who offered them, with subjects upon whom they might vent their ferocious instincts, we might, if we wished to pursue the system of interpreting the woods religion from a hygienic point of view, reverse Lancisi's argument, and say that the god Esus of Gaul and the Nemorense Diana of the Latins, were myths of the malaria produced in the groves dedicated to those divinities. But the hygienic question cannot be dragged in, for this simple reason, that in the mountains of Auvergne malaria has never been known to exist, and Genzano has always been salubrious, and continues to be so to this day.

This great hygienic argument, deduced from the veneration of groves in ancient times, can therefore, as has been shown, have no value whatever in dealing with the question under consideration. Nor does it acquire any greater importance from the citation, that Lancisi makes of a passage from Lucanus, which states that at the siege of Marseille, the soldiers of Cæsar refused to cut down a sacred forest, and that Cæsar, in order to obtain the timber necessary for his siege operations, was obliged to set them the example himself, by setting to work with a hatchet.

> . . . . "librare bipennem
> Ansus et aeriam ferro proscindere quercum."

From what historical source Lucanus obtained the anecdote it is impossible to say. Certainly not from Cæsar. Cæsar, who never missed the opportunity, even in his Commentaries on the Civil War, of mentioning the difficulties which he encountered on various occasions, from the ill-temper, the prejudices, and the unreliability of his soldiers, makes no allusion to this serious difficulty which he is said to have met with before Marseille. On the contrary, he mentions the cutting of timber incidentally, saying that he arrived before Marseille with three legions, executed the operations of approach, and in addition built twelve galleys, which were ready for sea, and manned in thirty days, dating from the day of the trees being felled. And this felling, of which he speaks so cursorily, was no mean undertaking. for shortly after, when Cæsar relates the burning of the besieging works through the treachery of the inhabitants of Marseille, during a truce, he says that it was necessary to line the new trenches with bricks for want of timber, all the trees in the neighbourhood of Marseille having been already cut down. But, even admitting that Lucanus was better acquainted with what happened at the siege of Marseille than Cæsar himself, and that the legionaries feared to touch a sacred forest, that would only prove that they believed it to be consecrated to a revengeful and dangerous divinity. Even at this distance of time, it may safely be asserted that the last idea which troubled them was concerning the effects which the cutting down of the trees might have had on the salubrity of Marseille and its neighbourhood.

From the historical arguments of Lancisi, of which I have quoted the only one deserving of any notice, let us proceed to his scientific ones. As he was far from supposing that the malaria of Cisterna proceeded from the land surrounding that town, but instead had a rooted idea that the unhealthiness of Cisterna, and eventually of Rome, was due to the malaria of the Pontine marshes being carried along by winds, it was only natural that he should fix upon the sirocco as the incriminated wind. As a matter of fact the situation of Cisterna with respect to the Pontine marshes is in the line of that wind. Still a great difficulty had to be overcome before admitting that the forest to the south of Cisterna could hinder the malaria from reaching that city. Cisterna is 77 metres above the level of the sea. and the Caetani's forest was at a much lower level, leaving the problem to be solved, as to how this forest, situated at a lower level, could possibly filter the atmospheric currents on their way towards a higher region. Probably some advocate on behalf of the Caetani did raise the objection; for, after the first discourse pronounced by Lancisi before the Commission, there are evident signs that he took great pains to clear up this point. He got out of the difficulty in a very simple manner. He invented a meteorological axiom, which is one of the most ludicrous things that ever entered the mind of a student of natural history, and assuming it to be a proved fact, made it the scientific basis of his opinion. It is well to quote its actual words, for were any one to put forward in his own language such a statement, he would lay himself open to the charge of defaming the venerated memory of Lancisi.

"The Austral winds and their collaterals are of a special nature and entirely different from the northern winds: that is to say, the south winds spring from downwards, and scouring the plains of the earth, rise up towards the mountains: whereas the north winds, starting from above, blow downwards and press the underlying earth. This fact does not seem to have been noticed by the common people, and to have been overlooked by some of our scientific writers."

I do not know whether there existed in Lancisi's time writers of physical meteorology capable of asserting that currents of hot air, rarefied and light, penetrate into our temperate atmosphere, skimming the soil over which they pass, and also on the other hand, that currents of cold and heavy air penetrate into this same atmosphere at a great height and far above the soil. Let us hope not, for the honour of science; for Galileo, Newton, and the Accademia del Cimento, had flourished in the previous century, and it is difficult to believe that a writer on physics would, in the eighteenth century, attempt to upset the laws of gravity simply to suit his fancy. As to the common people, it was impossible to expect from them such an unpractical observation, inasmuch as the experience of ages had taught them the exact opposite to Lancisi's theory. There is not a peasant in the southern parts of Italy who cannot foretell the approach of the sirocco several hours before its arrival; for they *see* the sirocco long before it begins to make itself felt. The heated and rarefied current of the sirocco enters into our atmosphere at an immense height, and announces its approach by an opaque veil which spreads itself over the uppermost atmosphere, and which is easily seen by day; by night its presence is revealed by the trembling of the stars. It is only much later on, when the temperature of the local atmosphere and that of the sirocco have become equalized, that the current descends and is felt. Naturally it is felt sooner in the higher regions than on the plains. In order to filtrate the malaria carried along by such a current, forests formed of the gigantic sequoia of California would not suffice, although they are said to attain a much greater height than the dome of St. Peter's. In fact in Rome the sirocco currents, although they meet on the way, the forests of the littoral and the Latial mountains as well, arrive in the city still laden with the sands of Africa, which have frequently been collected at the Roman Observatory. It must be conceded, therefore, that if those filters and barriers are not able to free the sirocco of the particles of sand, they can scarcely be expected to clear it of the minute germs of the malaria.

Instead of taking those facts into consideration, Lancisi, infatuated with the idea of upholding his theory, found it more convenient to make the sirocco currents enter from below, to make them skim along the shores of the littoral so as to oblige them to filter themselves in the forests lying on their way, and to make them reach the higher regions only after they had thus been purged and cleansed; and, with the weight of his authority, he succeeded not only in preventing the Caetani from cutting down their forest, but in having a law established which, contrary to what happens in all other parts of the world, has not served to protect the mountain forests of the Province of Rome, but to perpetuate a chain of forests in the plains.

Such an outrage on common sense and experience struck me very forcibly, from the time that I first took up the study of Roman malaria: nor were even the reasons adduced by Lancisi, such as to make me think better of it. There were so many and telling facts showing its absurdity, that the only difficulty was one of choice when I undertook to expose that legislative error. But the forest of Cisterna which had been the cause of the law-suit in 1714, furnished me with the most important evidence. About thirty years ago the Caetani cut it all down, and transformed into pasture and arable fields, the region which it occupied in the south. Ever since then the atmosphere of Cisterna began to improve, and by degrees that town, which was becoming depopulated, commenced to assume a new life. I do not say that Cisterna has become as healthy a place as Albano or Frascati, but only, that it is much more salubrious than formerly, and that the appearance of its population, as well as the death rates, bear ample testimony to the fact.

I verified this state of things on the spot in 1879, and made the fact public. As was to be expected, such a want of respect for the authority of Lancisi gave rise to many noisy denials which, however, produced some useful results. Miceli, the then Minister of Agriculture, was induced by it to undertake a close study of the question, and for that purpose appointed a Commission, which for three years has scoured the whole of the province of Rome, in order to arrive at a correct opinion. After three years of a steady and conscientious study of places, that Commission presented its report to the Minister, in which all the facts collected are minutely set forth; and the unanimous conclusions arrived at, placed the theory of Lancisi at its true value. It will be sufficient to extract from that report the most important of those conclusions—the second :—

FORESTS AND THE ROMAN MALARIA. 111

"The Commission in all its visits and from inquiries made in every place within the province of Rome, where sanitary reports, appeals from parishes, and statements published during the last eighty years, declare that the total or partial destruction of forests, woods, or groves had caused an increase of malaria, has not been able to find any proof of such deplorable consequences, but, on the contrary, that the opposite has often been the result. In fact, in those places where woods had been destroyed or circumscribed, malaria has not increased, but in some places it has diminished."

One of the members of that Commission, Professor Tacchini, director of the Observatory at the Collegio Romano, has added as an appendix to that document, a meteorological report of the province of Rome, which is of the highest importance as regards the effect of winds upon the salubrity of that region. In the following table I have shown the principal figures of that most interesting paper, which deals with the twelve years from the end of 1870 till the end of 1882:—

Year.	Average of Rainfall during the Months of March, April, and May.	Percentage of Fever in the Province of Rome during the Third Quarter of the Year.	Number of Days during the Third Quarter of the Year in which the sirocco prevailed.	Frequency of Northerly Winds during the Months of July, August, and September.	Average of Maximum Temperature during the Months of July and August.	Amount of Nebulosity during the Months of June, July, and August.
1871	185·8 m.m.	6·4	4	0·370	30·3 C.	2·3
1872	251·3 ,,	7·1	5	0·328	30·0	2·5
1873	187·7 ,,	7·3	5	0·372	32·1	2·0
1874	225·8 ,,	5·5	3	0·415	30·0	2·7
1875	258·7 ,,	6·2	3	0·341	30·0	2·9
1876	205·0 ,,	4·6	2	0·370	29·9	2·8
1877	191·9 ,,	4·2	8	0·311	31·0	2·7
1878	101·8 ,,	2·9	10	0·337	30·0	3·5
1879	369·9 ,,	11·4	4	0·335	29·8	1·8
1880	209·8 ,,	8·2	5	0·335	30·6	3·2
1881	227·3 ,,	6·6	4	0·196	31·7	2·7
1882	115·7 ,,	2·5	11	0·200	29·4	3·0

The unhealthy quarter of the year in the province of Rome is the third (July, August, and September), during which malaria attains its greatest development. The third column of the table gives the percentage of fever existing amongst the population of the province during that quarter, in each consecutive year from 1870 till 1882. The fourth column shows the number of ascertained times of the sirocco blowing during that same period. If we compare the figures in those two columns, we find that the sirocco blew most frequently in the years 1878 and 1882, during which, there was the least percentage of fever. This is the exact contrary to what is generally believed —that is, that the sirocco brings malaria into the region of Rome, either from the marshes of Africa or from those on the littoral. Moreover, the table shows that the largest percentage of fever happened in 1879; a year during the dangerous quarter of which, there were only a few days on which the sirocco blew.

If we were to reason in the same way as the faddists do—that is to say, by bringing forward only such facts as bear upon one side of the question, and omitting those which tell against it—the figures of those two columns would be sufficient to justify the assertion that the sirocco, contrary to Lancisi's theory, instead of bringing malaria, rather impedes its development. But that would be making as foolish a use of facts as Lancisi did. The sirocco, of itself, neither brings malaria nor does it hinder its development, but, under certain circumstances, rather favours it. Everything depends upon the hygrometric condition of the land, when the sirocco blows over it. If the malaria-producing soil is dry, the increase of temperature caused by the sirocco is in no wise injurious; but, should it be in a humid condition, then the increase of temperature caused by the sirocco acts as a co-efficient in the malaria production.

An examination of the figures in the second column of the table shows that in the two years 1878 and 1882, during which, there was the smallest average of fever and the greatest of sirocco winds, there fell also the least amount of spring rain in the twelve years. During those two years the heat of the summer was excessive, and the malarious lands were dry, or almost so; the development of malaria was therefore at its lowest point, although the sirocco winds were most prevalent. In 1879, on the contrary, the spring rainfall reached the highest point in the twelve years' period, and the outbreak of malaria was also the strongest, although there was but a small amount of sirocco winds; because, when the summer heat arrived, the malarious lands of the province of Rome still retained a large quantity of humidity.

Surgeon-Colonel Giudici, ever since 1872, has drawn attention to the fact, that the outbreak of fever in the province of Rome, has no direct relation with the increase of temperature during the summer months. And that is true. During July, 1879, there were many cold days, and, as the figures in the sixth column of the table show, the average of the highest temperature of the summer of 1879 (during which there was the greatest percentage of fever for the period 1871-82) was nearly the same, as the average recorded for 1882, the year in which the percentage of fever was reduced to its lowest point. It is often said that northerly winds would exercise a beneficial effect in this region during the fever season, and that it would be very advantageous to deforest all the mountains lying to the north of the Agro Romano, in order to allow a free scope to their beneficent action. It is natural that those who own woods on those mountains should be in favour of such a theory, in order not to have to contend with the Italian forestal law, as an impediment to their making a rapid fortune; but in truth there is nothing

I

to justify the idea. The fifth column of the table tells us that during the period 1871-82 northerly winds prevailed to an equal extent, during the third quarter of the years 1879 and 1878—that is to say, in the year when there was the greatest percentage of fever, and in one of the two years when it was lowest.

The production of fever in the Agro Romano and in Rome cannot be attributed to any one or other single cause. It is the result of a combination of meteorological and physiological facts. A free development of malaria in this region, only takes place when its numerous malarious grounds are both damp and overheated. The amount of malaria in the atmosphere breathed by the inhabitants who live there may vary greatly, according to the proportions in which the two indispensable factors of the malaria development in a malarious soil,—heat and humidity exposed to the air,—are blended together. If those two factors should be at their highest point, the malaria-load of the atmosphere is at its greatest, especially when the sky is serene. It would seem in fact, that the figures of the seventh column of the table, which I have drawn up from data supplied by Tacchini, denote a certain relation between the increase of the nebulosity of the atmosphere and the diminution in its malarious quality. It may be, that the nebulosity of the atmosphere does produce that diminution, by tempering the effect of the sun's action upon the malarious lands ; or it may be, that it produces that result, because it reduces the calorific radiation of the soil, and thereby, diminishes the rising into the atmosphere of the malarious germs contained in the soil. When the atmosphere has been in a state of malarious saturation for many consecutive days, and the systems of the inhabitants have been more or less penetrated with malarious germs, the lowering of the temperature may produce a most detrimental effect (as will be shown further on), because it conduces to the retention of those germs in the system, and prevents their quick discharge from the body by means of the secretions. Hence it is, that the action of northerly winds during the fever season, is very often, anything but favourable. On the other hand, it most frequently happens that the southerly winds, and even the sirocco, the hottest of all, blow, without producing any noxious effect, since they do not carry malaria of themselves, or at least they carry it in such a scattered state as not to be able to produce infection in the human body; and again, when the malarious lands are in a dry state, they cannot induce the production of malaria simply by raising, as they do, the temperature of the soil.

A proper study of the facts, although such a study has only been undertaken within the last few years, enables us to demolish the whole of Lancisi's theory as to the part played by the north and south winds, and also as to the necessary filtration of the latter by means of shore forests. That theory has had the most disastrous effects upon the province of Rome; because, whilst it has contributed to the destruction of mountain forests, which might have been useful in regulating the waters of that region, it has led to the preservation of forests situated in low-lying malarious grounds, where they can only be productive of harm. Even recently, when the Chigis desired to free the pinewood of Castel Fusaro, situated on the littoral of Ostia, from the old forestal conditions, their request was refused, because it was asserted that that pinewood preserved that region from malarious importations. But from where? To maintain that that pinewood filters the malaria coming from Africa is absurd; and still more absurd is the idea that it preserves the Agro and Rome from the pestilential emanations of the swamp of Ostia, for it is situated between the sea and the swamp of Ostia, and not between the latter and the Agro. That the preservation of that splendid pinewood should be desired on æsthetical grounds is right enough; but to insist upon its preservation, for hygienic reasons, is an outrage on common sense.

But this is not all. Inasmuch as a fundamental error always breeds others of minor importance, that idea of woods acting as filters to the malaria has been the cause of spoiling the finest of the new streets of Rome. When the Via Nazionale was commenced, which starts from the Piazza di Termini, trees were planted all along the footpath. But when the plantation had reached the intersection by the Via delle Quattro Fontane, a new inspector of public works was appointed by the municipality of Rome, who reasoned in this manner:—" The leaves of trees retain the malaria carried along by the winds; malaria does not come to Rome except by means of winds from without; therefore it would be madness to plant trees in Rome, for they would act as so many condensers of malaria." And as he was a man of strong convictions, he determined to preserve the city from any such harm in the future; and in order that it should not enter into any one's head to continue the planting of trees along the Via Nazionale, he made that impossible, by constructing the sewers of the street on the line of the plantation which had already been begun. Owing to this, the Via Nazionale has been deprived of trees, to the great discomfort of those who have to pass along it during the summer, for, as it runs from east to west, it is exposed to the rays of the sun during nearly the whole of the day.

Let us now hope that after the publication of the report of the Commission of 1881 such ideas will disappear, and that in our laws no further mention will be made of a forestal barrier along the plains. But we must not be very sanguine in such a hope. Prejudices die hard, and rather than read a book of 142 pages, furnished with statistical maps and tables which require an attentive study, most persons prefer to believe in ancient traditions, and satisfy themselves by saying "*Lancisi says so, and therefore it must be correct.*" The dogmatic assertions of persons of authority have always the effect of throwing back the progress of scientific investigations for a considerable time, because they are blindly accepted by people who shut their eyes to the most evident facts.

The history of the discovery of the circulation of the blood affords a striking example of this. From the time of Galen, who asserted that the blood flowed from one ventricle of the heart into another by means of pores existing in the septum which separates the two ventricles, till that of Realdo Colombo, who proved by experiment, that that septum was impervious, and that the blood passed from the right to the left ventricle by means of the pulmonary circulation, thirteen centuries elapsed. During all those centuries anatomists endeavoured to find the perforations described by Galen, but without success, and they confessed that they were not to be seen; still they accepted the statement, alleging that they must exist, because Galen had said so. Even the great Vesalius took refuge in such a mode of reasoning, until the day of the convincing discovery by Realdo Colombo. Nor did the Galen prejudice cease to prevail, even after Colombo's conclusive demonstrations. Cesalpino himself, who is wrongly considered in Italy as the discoverer of the great circulation, insisted upon recognizing the pores described by Galen, even though Colombo had proved several years before, that they did not exist. The Lancisi prejudice may prevail for a while longer, but it will not last as long as the Galen prejudice, because in the present day the scientific world progresses more rapidly than formerly, and draws along with it the educated classes, with greater success than in times gone by. Perhaps in some ten or twenty years it will appear an unjustifiable and strange thing that, at this present moment, I should have spent so many arguments in combating an arbitrary dictum of 1714, founded upon an error in physics which no student of our lyceums would dare to advocate.

CHAPTER VII.

THE PERMANENT SANITATION OF THE AGRO ROMANO.

ALL the economical and industrial interests which are now concentrated in Rome are striving, with a determination unknown since the fall of the Roman Empire, to discover, if possible, the means of effectually suppressing the production of malaria in the district surrounding the new capital of Italy.

The conviction that this morbific agent is not imported into the Agro nor into Rome from distant marshes, but breaks forth into the atmosphere from almost every part of the Roman soil, gains ground every day in public opinion, and, in spite of school prejudices, begins to be accepted in preference to the theories which have prevailed hitherto. On the other hand, confidence diminishes every day, in the idea of being able to effect any definitive sanitation of the soil by means of a simple hydraulic improvement, not only, because it has already been brought home to some, that the difficulties in the way of effecting a complete hydraulic improvement of this territory, are enormous, but especially because all those who have any practical experience in matters relating to the Roman Campagna, know that the effects of the most perfect system of hydraulic sanitation are liable to be easily compromised by a rainy season. It is only natural, therefore, that attention should have been devoted to the finding of a means of suppressing the production of malaria in the Roman soil once for all, and of obtaining a permanent sanitation which atmospheric changes cannot destroy. This aim is natural, and useful as well, but upon the one condition, that assiduous care and attentive study should be brought to bear upon the most likely means of obtaining such a result, and that no crude plans should be adopted which, whilst furthering the interests of a few individuals, would by no means tend to any public advantage.

When we talk of the permanent sanitation of malarious land, we mean that its composition should be modified in such a manner as to render it sterile as regards the malaria-ferment, but at the same time, preserving its capacity for furnishing products useful to social economy. To obtain this desirable result with certainty, it is necessary in the first place, to know exactly what a cultivable soil should be composed of, so as to be incapable of producing malaria: and having ascertained that point, then, this further question has to be solved,—what are the practical means of imparting that composition to the soil which it is proposed to redeem from malaria? Unfortunately, it is this very point of departure which still remains to be discovered. At present, we are ignorant of what the composition of a cultivable soil ought to be, in order to render it incapable of producing malaria. Hence it is, that we do not know what ought to be done to render unproductive of malaria, any one of the numerous soils which contain the malaria-ferment. Neither science nor experience has as yet given us the slightest clue towards a solution of this problem.

From this, it is easy to infer how great are the difficulties, which the problem of the permanent sanitation of the Roman district presents, where not one, but ever so many are the cultivable soils which offer an excellent field for the production of malaria. If no one can conscientiously suggest a means of rendering permanently unproductive, so far as malaria is concerned, any single species of cultivable ground, how can it be asserted, that we are able to produce that specific sterility in the Roman territory, where the complications of the geological structure and of the underground hydrography have multiplied the variety of malarious soils to so great an extent? But, if those who have studied this problem for years, and who have learnt from that prolonged study, this one thing for certain—that our ignorance on this particular point is far greater than could have been imagined—shrink from making any such assertion; it is far otherwise with those who know nothing on the subject. At various intervals, plans for the permanent sanitation of the Agro Romano, have been put forward; some extravagant and absurd, and others dangerous from an economico-social point of view; but all equally arbitrary.

First of all, appeared the sunflower system. Many years ago, it was suggested that an immense quantity of sunflowers should be planted all over the Agro Romano, in order to destroy the production of malaria. The sunflowers were to perform a double function: to modify the composition of the ground in which they were planted, and to attract on to the Agro, with their great abundance of seeds, clouds of birds, which flying about in the air in every direction should purify the atmosphere of malaria. From where the idea came that the sunflower plant had any useful influence on a malarious soil, it is impossible to imagine; and still less so, the notion that birds swallowed up the malaria. According to that idea, the Coliseum, which is full of birds of all kinds, ought to be the healthiest spot in Rome, whereas in fact, it is one of the most unhealthy. Anyhow, the idea took; and many can remember seeing, in passing through the Agro Romano, numerous plantations of sunflowers, especially in the neighbourhood of railway stations and roadkeepers' cottages.

The fashion for sunflowers was succeeded by that for eucalyptus trees. As usual, the notion was, that in the case of the Agro, we had to deal with a marshy plain, and the eucalyptus trees were expected to perform three different sanitary functions at the same time. They were to absorb the water from the swamps, and produce a hydraulic improvement; also to destroy, with the aroma of their leaves, the malaria contained in the atmosphere; and finally, to choke the production of malaria in the ground, by a layer formed of their dead leaves falling upon it. Those leaves, sodden by water, were to produce the desired specific sterility in the soil, by moistening it continually with an anti-malarial liquid, formed of the watery infusion of these healing leaves.

From those innocent fancies, we arrive at suggestions which might have been productive of hygienic disasters or of economical misfortunes. Some people, who imagined that the Agro Romano was a flat surface, like the plains of Lombardy, thought they could ameliorate its hygienic and agricultural condition by means of a superficial system of irrigation. I need not stop to consider the value of that idea, as regards agricultural economy. Common sense leads us at once to observe, that we are not dealing with the plains of Lombardy, but with an extent of land, the reverse of flat, and that, as far as concerns those portions of it which are flat, irrigation without any profitable result has been carried on in bygone times on a vast scale. In the valley of Arrone, for example, there are a number of farms (Santa Maria di Galicia, San Giacomo, Boccea, Testa di Lepre, and Leprignana), where numerous stalls may be found in which draught oxen are kept. Those stalls were not originally built for such cattle, but were erected for Swiss milch cows, which at one time were bred in great numbers in the meadows of the valley of the Arrone, which were duly irrigated for that purpose. But that undertaking was abandoned, chiefly because it proved non-remunerative. I cannot say whether such a result was occasioned by the pasturage not being sufficiently abundant, in spite of the systematic irrigation, or because the cows suffered from attacks of malaria. I simply mention the fact that it was abandoned by all the owners and tenants of that district, notwithstanding the considerable amount of capital which they had invested to ensure its success. It does not seem to me a very encouraging precedent for those agriculturists who wish to renew the experiment.

As regards the hygienic effects of irrigations on the Agro, we have no facts to induce us to believe that they will prove advantageous; on the contrary, what we do know inclines us to suppose that they will be disastrous. In support of this view it is sufficient to recall to mind, what has already been noticed, respecting the connection which exists between the production of malaria and the rainfall, to prove its probability. The irrigation of the Agro during the hot weather would most likely have no other result, than that of increasing the production of malaria. Any one who has a practical knowledge of the Agro is aware that in many spots, malaria has been known to increase whenever the experiment of making irrigated gardens has been tried. Even in Rome, there was a striking instance when, after 1870, large tracts of the Cœlius were turned into irrigated kitchen gardens. The Cœlian hill was always unhealthy, as long as its soil remained uncovered, and it is only now, since new buildings have begun to invade that region, that the atmosphere has commenced to improve. But the unhealthiness of the Cœlius increased in an unusual manner, when a great portion of its surface was occupied by those kitchen gardens, and did not return to its normal state until they were removed. The fixed population in the hospital of S. Giovanni felt those alternations of local malaria very strongly; and certainly this example does not recommend the introduction of irrigated cultivations in the Agro Romano.

It remains to be seen whether other kinds of cultivation, different from those actually in vogue in the Campagna, may not produce a permanent sanitation of that region. From all that is said and written on the subject in Italy and abroad, it would appear that it is a settled matter, and admits of no doubt. And the confidence with which the fact is asserted by so many, that the transformation of the Roman meadows into highly-cultivated fields will drive malaria for ever from that region, makes it appear strange that there should be so many others who do not blindly believe it. Perhaps, however, that surprise will be greatly lessened after hearing a full statement of the facts.

It will be advisable, in the first place, to go into the history of the idea—for that idea of the complete transformation of the cultivation of the Agro has a history, and not a very edifying one. Some, indeed, have put forward the notion in perfect good faith, allowing themselves to be persuaded by preconceived theories and authoritative statements, whereas, others have had in view, objects totally unconnected with the public weal. The great fuss which was made after the end of the year 1870, respecting the obligation incumbent upon the Italian Government to take immediate steps, at any cost, for the sanitation of the Agro Romano, brought forth speculators from every country. The first points insisted upon were three: the necessity of making a radical change in the cultivation of the Agro; the impossibility of carrying out that change so long as the actual owners were in possession; and the duty of providing a legal means of eviction. It sufficed to pass a law prescribing a certain kind of cultivation for the Agro Romano, as a matter of public benefit, and then to appropriate for the public benefit the property of all those who refused to comply with those prescriptions.

Until 1883, the speculative crowd did not despair of getting such a law passed. There was a time, between 1880 and 1883, when these expectations ran so high, that the speculators were imprudently led to expose their aim. The plan was a very simple one. If they could succeed in getting a law passed, insisting upon certain modes of cultivation being adopted, which the proprietors of the Agro Romano might find too burdensome to accept, their forcible eviction would be the natural result. The Italian Government would have had thrown on its hands an immense quantity of land charged with the obligation of a fixed method of cultivation, already declared to be impracticable, unless at a ruinous cost, by the owners of the soil. In order to get rid of the burden, the Italian authorities would have been constrained to accept the smallest offers, and the intending buyers hoped, not only to buy the land very cheaply, but also to impose upon the Government the condition, that penitentiary colonies should be established at different places in this region, so as to reduce the cost of cultivation.

There is no exaggeration in that statement. If we wish to see how the questions of hygiene are occasionally made use of by the most audacious speculators, we need only read the newspapers and publications of that time, and there we shall find set out that financial scheme in a clear and striking light. The "*redeemer of the Agro Romano*" became a type of philanthropic swindler, well known throughout Europe, and has already found a place in modern literature.* And in expectation of the passing of

* See the English novel, "Madame de Presnel," by E. Frances Poynter.

that law, which was to open out such a useful field of operations to this new race of speculators, companies were formed in different localities for the sanitation of the Agro Romano, one of which, the notorious "Banque Romaine," in Belgium, succeeded in getting itself greatly talked about in the financial world, but failed, before the much-desired law was even discussed.

That law was laid before the Chamber of Deputies in 1883, and it was discussed and passed, the same year. It obliged the owners of lands situated within a radius of ten kilometres from the golden milestone of the Roman Forum, to execute certain works which were considered conducive to the sanitation of the Agro Romano. The Chamber, however, fully apprised by what has already been narrated of the grasping nature of some benefactors, excluded all possible intervention on the part of speculating companies, and undertook to protect the public welfare whilst safeguarding, at the same time, the legitimate interests of the landowners. It was decreed that all proposals of improvement should emanate from the landowners themselves: that they should lay those proposals before a Commission appointed for the purpose: that the Commission, after having duly examined them, should either accept or reject them, and in the latter case produce counter-proposals. In the event of a divergence of views between the land owners and the Commission, the proposals of the former and the counter-proposals of the latter were to be discussed by the Superior Council of Agriculture, before which, both sides could appear in support of their respective views, ere the Government decided upon a compulsory mode of sanitation.

Thus, projects which were simply theoretical, were put aside; for the interested parties, and the Government as well, were placed under the necessity of studying in each instance, the hydrographical and geological conditions of the various localities proposed for sanitation, and were driven to formulate their plans and counterplans with a due regard to those conditions. Hence it is to be hoped that, during the progress of this vast undertaking, the projects of those dreamers who seek to improve the Agro Romano, whilst sitting at their desks, without having the slightest practical knowledge of the country, will be rejected; and that at the same time the vile speculations of many swindlers will fall to the ground.

Amongst the numerous proposed solutions, the one which has found the greatest amount of public support, is to exclude the malaria from the Agro by cutting up that region into small holdings, and substituting the close cultivation of these for the extensive cultivation of large farms. If that were a certain remedy, the malaria ought to have disappeared, or at any rate to be greatly reduced, in that part of the Agro where that change has already been carried out—that is to say, in the zone immediately surrounding Rome. The suburban district of Rome contains a superficies of 7,500 hectares, which are divided amongst 1,200 owners. The average, therefore, of each owner is about six hectares; but in reality, as Poggi has proved, many of them only possess half a hectare, one, two, or five hectares—the number of those who own twenty, or more than twenty, hectares is exceedingly small. Throughout the whole of that district, extreme cultivation is carried out, and consists of vines, olives, and vegetables. And yet it is well known, that in many of those holdings malaria is quite as prevalent, and more so sometimes, than in some of the large farms of the Agro.

It is probable that the extreme cultivation of the soil, combined with the hydraulic improvement of the same, may in some cases have succeeded in destroying for ever, the malarious production existing in it. But in many cases, its disappearance was only apparent and not real; it was in fact, only an interruption of the pestilential product, which lasted as long only as the labour of cultivation was continuous, but ceased the moment the fields became neglected. Many of the sanitations effected in ancient times in Italian territories, and especially in the Agro Romano, were not permanent but simply temporary.

Even such a partial result would be a great gain—and if we might be certain of it, we could undertake the close cultivation of the Agro, without stopping to consider whether the sanitation thus obtained would be permanent or simply temporary. But the misfortune is, that no one can predict the result with any certainty; and no one can say beforehand, whether the cultivation of a malarious tract will render it salubrious or not. It even occurs sometimes, that the cultivation of a malarious tract increases the production of malaria. In the beginning, that almost always happens; because when a malarious soil is turned up by the plough or by the spade, the surface of the soil in direct contact with the air is increased, and necessarily the development of malaria increases also. Popular experience has proved it, and continues to prove it every day, especially in Italy and America. The first noxious effect of cultivation often diminishes gradually with time, and sometimes disappears altogether. But at other times it continues persistently, and there are instances in which, from despair, the extreme cultivation has had to be abandoned, and the soil relevelled and coated over, so to say, with close pasturage, in order to render it less pestilential.

On the other hand, it must be admitted that it is impossible to say, *à priori*, that this first lamentable effect of extreme cultivation will not disappear in the course of time, and that a sanitation of the cultivated tract may not take place. It is entirely a matter of chance; and neither science nor experience gives any clue to the final result. In the Agro Romano, this chance is still more risky than in other malarious localities, owing to the multiplicity of complications in its geological structure and in its hydrographical conditions; as well as to the tenacity which the malarious production has displayed in many places of the Agro Romano, where close cultivation had been so long carried on, in the past.

In the absence of any positive knowledge, it is evident that no unremunerative cultivation of the Agro Romano could be authoritatively decreed, with a hygienic object in view. It might be enforced, provided there were a certainty that any given method of cultivation would produce the sanitation of the malarious lands; because, in that case, the pecuniary sacrifice which the owners might refuse to incur, might in justice be thrown upon the national rates, after the eviction had taken place, as it would be a real benefit conferred upon the capital of Italy. But, since this certainty of the hygienic effect does not exist, it would be a crying injustice, to carry out at the expense of the landowners in the Roman district, or of the ratepayers of Italy, after the eviction of the former, an experiment, from which no certain hygienic result can be predicted, and which might ensure a serious financial loss to either the former or the latter.

I am not induced to express myself in this way, by theoretical ideas. Amongst the many things which are thoughtlessly said respecting the Agro Romano, the one which is most frequently repeated is this: that the soil of the Agro is extremely fertile, and that it might easily be converted into one of the richest agricultural districts of Italy. But as a fact, the productiveness of the Roman soil is very limited, much more so than might be generally believed. Even when the vegetable soil was much more abundant than it is now after all the diminution it has suffered, (of which I have spoken in the second chapter), this portion of Italy was not celebrated for its fertility. To prove this, we may appeal to the lamentation of the Roman legionaries after the retaking of Capua, which Livy has recorded, and which has already been quoted in a former chapter. The legionaries did not confine themselves, according to the narrative, with comparing the salubrity of the Agro Campano with the unhealthiness of the Agro Romano, but dwelt upon the vast difference which existed between the great fertility of the one, and the scant productiveness of the other. From this we may reasonably infer that Livy himself, who wrote three centuries after the taking of Capua, did not have a very exalted idea of the fertility of the Agro Romano.

Some recent instances of the extreme cultivation of the Agro Romano have shown such results as ought to recommend great circumspection in suggesting or enforcing a change in the cultivation of that region. It will be sufficient to quote the instance of the Tre Fontane farm. It has already been mentioned in a former chapter, under what exceptionally favourable circumstances the experiment of a change in the mode of cultivation was attempted there. The land was leased by the Trappist monks at a very low price, and manual labour was guaranteed to them by the presence of a convict colony during the whole year, at a minimum cost, with every facility of payment. Besides, all the expenses of lodging, of victuals, of clothing, of overlooking, of hospitals, and of the replacement of sick hands, were defrayed by the Government. But, in spite of such unusual advantages, that agricultural speculation was not a success; and it is no longer a secret, that it was only preserved from total failure, because the greater portion of the land had not been put under cultivation; and also because on the property leased there existed a rich quarry of pozzolana and tufa, which, whilst there was so much activity in building operations at Rome, produced a sufficient return, to cover the losses of the agricultural speculations then in hand.

There can be no question as to the fact that the malaria of the Agro constitutes one of the principal drawbacks to the introduction there, of those methods of cultivation which require the presence of man on the spot during the whole year. But it may be surely asserted, that this is not the only obstacle, nor even the principal one, very often. The agricultural population of Southern Italy is ready to expose itself to the malaria, either in Italy or abroad, with great courage, provided it can secure a money return; and a large part of the Agro Romano would be more thickly populated than it actually is, even in spite of the malaria, if the nature of the soil were less ungrateful. The case of the Pontine marshes proves this; inasmuch as malaria is much more virulent there than in the Agro Romano, but the soil is much more fertile. At the foot of the hill upon which Sezze, the ancient *Setia*, is built, in the so-called "Campi Setini," a close cultivation is carried on by the inhabitants of Sezze. They are decimated by the malaria to such an extent, that it is unusual to find one of their women who has not had three or four husbands, because the town of Sezze itself is comparatively healthy, and it is only the male portion of the population who go down to the fields to work. They pay a heavy tribute to the malaria, but they still persist, because the money return from the cultivation of the "Campi Setini" is very considerable. Such is not the case in the Agro Romano, and in many places of this region, where the masses of tufa being scarcely covered by the thinnest layer of vegetable earth, or being entirely bare, any attempt at intensive cultivation would prove economically disastrous.

After all, should the greater portion of the Agro Romano remain, as must be the case from the force of circumstances, covered by pasturage, which at any rate admits of the remunerative rearing of cattle during eight months of the year, the hygienic conditions of the Campagna will not suffer. Provided that the waters of these lands are well regulated, the meadows will, in this case, as elsewhere, constitute a form of atmospheric sanitation of the malarious soil, which has on many occasions been of great use.

No doubt, it would be well to introduce in the Agro, close cultivation wherever it can be adopted with a sure economical profit, not only for reasons of social advantage, which every one can appreciate, but also because it is just possible, that in course of time it may produce a permanent sanitation. No one can say that any advantage will be derived from it, but on the other hand no one can say that it will not produce some good; because it is well known that in some malarious places it has contributed considerably to sanitation. It is entirely a question of chance, as has already been shown; but, whenever the local conditions are favourable to its adoption, without exposing the cultivators to certain loss, or rather by offering them a probability of gain, then the risk may be incurred without doing injustice to any one.

But I repeat, that even under such favourable conditions, neither science nor the practical experience of malaria which we have as yet acquired, promises any certainty of obtaining a permanent sanitation. The only hygienic benefit which such a change in the cultivation of the Agro can be reckoned on producing, is the improvement and maintenance in good order, of the hydraulic condition of the tracts placed under close cultivation. Wherever a moderate profit may induce small proprietors, or families of agriculturists, to settle down permanently in such parts of the Agro Romano as are recognized to be capable of close cultivation, persons will be found who are interested in improving and maintaining the hydraulic sanitation, which ought to be the principal base of all agricultural improvements in the Campagna. This may appear a very small result to obtain in comparison with the total extinction of the Roman malaria, which so many persons in Italy and abroad are ready to promise with certainty. But it is the only benefit which can be assured, in the actual state of the knowledge which we possess; still it is not so very unimportant after all. In previous chapters the question of the enormous difficulties with which the complete hydraulic sanitation of the Agro is beset, has been fully dealt with. Everything, therefore, which tends to render its realization less slow and less imperfect, is an appreciable advantage, and, for my part, I would greatly rejoice if the agricultural conditions of the Roman Campagna should be such, as to admit of that being done, throughout its entire extent.

In the meanwhile, in order to facilitate its success in those parts of the Campagna where the change of cultivation is possible, let us consider whether there are any means adapted to preserve from attacks of malaria, those persons who may make it their permanent habitation. When the question of introducing close cultivation into malarious regions comes under consideration we, unfortunately, find ourselves travelling in a vicious circle, for the carrying out of close cultivation necessitates the permanent residence on the spot of the agriculturists during all the seasons of the year; whereas during one, at least, of those seasons, the danger to human life is too great to be encountered. The agricultural populations of Italy break through that vicious circle by courageously encountering the danger, whenever there is a prospect of commensurate gain. But they break it by paying an exorbitant tribute to the malaria, which consists not only in a greater or less sacrifice of human life, but likewise, in a gradual deterioration of the agricultural race. During these latter years in which the idea of colonising the Agro Romano has begun to be put into practice, I have been endeavouring to discover some means of escaping from that vicious circle, without occasioning the loss or the ruin, of so many lives. What I wished to arrive at, was to find whether it were not possible to render the human constitution less susceptible to attacks of malaria, by increasing its powers of resistance to that specific infection.

I hope that I have succeeded, at least partially, in finding a means of escape; and after all that has been said on the natural history of the Roman malaria, and on the little probability which exists, of seeing it extinguished during our lives, it will not appear unnatural, if I devote the last chapter on the "Climate of Rome" to the consideration of the knowledge which we so far possess, of the means adapted to preserve the lives of men from malarious infection. Such a study does not present much, if any, interest to those who inhabit the more crowded parts of Rome, and seldom emerge therefrom. But it may perhaps offer some interest, to those who live within the periphery of Rome, in the neighbourhood of turned up lands or of the excavations made for new buildings, and especially to those who are often called upon to travel through the Campagna during the hot season, or have to live there.

CHAPTER VIII.

THE PRESERVATION OF HUMAN LIFE IN MALARIOUS COUNTRIES.

From century to century the experience of people who have settled in malaria-producing countries, has taught them the possibility of avoiding, or at least of mitigating, the baneful effects of that morbific agent, by adopting certain precautions, which have become traditional. The analysis of those preventive measures, dictated by popular experience, shows that they were designed to realize two different objects—that is to say, to reduce as much as possible the quantity of the malaria-ferment which enters into the system through the air breathed; and to prevent a lengthened abode of the same in the system, into which it is introduced by every inhalation of the infected air.

It has already been shown that the atmosphere, which covers malaria-producing lands, is not equally laden with malaria during all the hours of the day. All other conditions being equal, that load is least during the mid-day hours, and greatest at the rising and setting of the sun. That fact has been recognized by popular experience, from time immemorial; and it is for that reason that, except in cases of necessity, the inhabitants of malarious countries avoid leaving their houses at sunrise or sunset. A people of wide celebrity, in Greco-Italian antiquity, namely the Sibarites, had adopted that knowledge as an axiom of public hygiene. The Sibarite proverb, "If you wish to live long and well, do not ever see the rising or the setting sun," is not, as is generally thought, a saying of the effeminate life which the wealthy Sibarites led in after times. It is the outcome of hard-bought experience, made by a people who had to live in a region so fiercely malarious as that in which Sibari was situated.

But, in addition to the discovery of the difference in the malaria-load of the local atmosphere, during various portions of the day, popular experience has acquired from remote times another important fact, throughout almost every quarter of the globe. It has proved that malaria rises to a limited height in a vertical direction, so that the malaria-load of the atmosphere, which covers a malaria-producing ground, becomes so reduced at a short distance above the soil, as to render its inhalation innocuous, or fraught with very little danger. Any one who visits the Pontine marshes may see in the open air, at different intervals, platforms erected upon poles four or five metres high, on which, in summer, people sleep during the night. To sleep in the open air during the fever season, in such a pestilential place as the Pontine marshes, appears at first sight an act of folly; nevertheless, experience proves that, under certain circumstances, it is not so. The requisite conditions are these—that the place selected should be so situated that the malaria cannot reach it from the original producing soil, except by means of vertical currents of air. These cannot succeed in poisoning the atmosphere with malaria, to a dangerous degree, except at a very limited height. In fact, what we see done in the Pontine marshes, by the people who sleep in the open air during the fever season, is repeated, in exactly the same form, in many malarious regions of Greece, and in the jungles of the East Indies. In both countries the system of wooden platforms slightly raised above the surface of the malarious soil is made use of to sleep in the open air during the night; or to watch for game, during a considerable length of time.

Probably the small dwellings placed on the summit of the tombs along the Via Appia and elsewhere, were erected with the same object; because the walls of those tombs rise perpendicularly from the surrounding Campagna. In Central and Southern America, the Indians, whenever they are driven to spend the night in malarious places, are in the habit of swinging their hammocks on the branches of the loftiest trees they can find. Perhaps, it was this custom of the Indians, which suggested to the engineers of the Panama Railway, (where the excavations produced an outbreak of malaria which destroyed several thousands of men), the idea of building little wooden huts on trees at a height of twenty or thirty feet from the ground.

Another practical way of utilizing this progressive diminution of the morbific power of the air above the surface of the malarious soil, is to construct the dwellings in such a way that, when the door is shut, the internal atmosphere is renewed only by the strata of the local atmosphere which are near the roofs of the houses. Some ancient farm buildings in the Campagna of Rome show how easily such a result can be obtained. At the Vienna Exposition of 1873 there was exhibited the model of an ancient farm building of a considerable size, from the Agro Romano, sent by Castellani, and illustrated by Tocco. In that house, the only opening in the outer walls was the door. All the windows looked into the inner yard, so that when the outside door was shut, the air of the yard and of the interior rooms could only be renewed by atmospheric strata situated at a higher level than the top of the roof. Here and there, on the Agro Romano, some ancient buildings have been discovered, which originally were very similar to that farm building. Some of those houses had no opening in the outer walls, save the principal door and small windows just under the eaves of the roof; so that, when the door was closed, the air in the interior was supplied only by the atmospheric strata which reached the spring of the roof. Even allowing that the principal aim of such a mode of construction was to ensure safety, it is plain that the objects, which the peasants of the Pontine marshes have in view, when they spend the night on their platforms, can easily be attained by it. Under such circumstances, immunity is almost certain, even though the distance between the surface of the malarious soil and the place of habitation be not great. The air thus breathed, does not contain malarious germs in such quantity, as to produce infection in the system of those who inhale it. The case is far different, when the places inhabited by human beings, are connected with the malarious soil, by means of inclined planes. Although the dwelling-place should be at a considerable elevation, malarious germs may reach it, by means of oblique ascending currents of air, in such a mass as easily to produce infection.

We have an example of this in the Pontine region. Along the slope of the Lepine mountains, which look towards the Pontine marshes, there are on the same line three small towns—Norma (the ancient *Norba*), Sermoneta, and Sezze. All these are exposed, in an identical manner, to the southerly winds, which, blowing over the marshes, reach those towns. According to the theory which asserts, that such winds bring the malaria of the Pontine marshes, and of the other sea-shore swamps into Rome, all those three towns ought to be equally affected by the miasma which those winds collect from the Pontine marshes. Such is not the case, however. Norma is perfectly healthy; Sezze not entirely; and Sermoneta, which lies between the two, is rendered uninhabitable by malaria.

The reason of the difference is this: that the malaria from the underlying marshes can only reach Norma by vertical currents of air; because Norma is connected with the Pontine marshes by a perpendicular rock; and thus, although it stands above Ninfa, one of the most pestilential spots in that region, the malaria does not reach up to it. Sezze is situated upon a hill fronting the marshes, with a less steep incline, and the malaria sometimes is found in certain parts of the town. Sermoneta lies on a height overlooking the marshes, with which it is connected by a gentle slope, along which the malaria of the marshes travels easily by means of oblique aërial currents, and reaches the town without having undergone any appreciable dispersion. Consequently, Sermoneta is becoming gradually depopulated. The much-vaunted sanitation of Pius VI. has only made matters worse, as regards that town, already sufficiently unprosperous owing to its unfortunate position with respect to the Pontine marshes.

All those various facts supplied by popular experience, regarding the manner in which malaria is distributed throughout the local atmosphere, might be applied to good purpose in Rome and in the Campagna. In Rome, in those houses which adjoin open grounds, and especially in those which adjoin grounds where excavations are being carried on, it would be well to keep the windows closed in the morning and during the early hours of the evening. This precaution is particularly recommended as regards the ground floors of those houses; it is of less consequence as regards the upper stories, because, in proportion to the height of the dwellings above the underlying soil, the atmosphere becomes less and less loaded with malarious exhalations. In the Campagna, and especially in those parts, where experience has shown that malaria is most pestilential, it would be advisable, that the internal atmosphere of the rooms should be drawn only from an interior court properly paved; that is to say, that no windows should be made in the external walls, or only in the highest story immediately under the roof when the houses are very high. For field watchers, moreover, wooden huts ought to be built on elevated platforms, and they should be so constructed, as to admit of easy removal, according to the rotation of agricultural operations, or the necessities of fresh cultivation.

It has been suggested, as a precautionary measure for sentries, railway watchers, revenue guards, convict guards, and in general for all those whose duties oblige them to remain in the Campagna, either stationary or patrolling on horseback, that they should wear respirators on their mouth, during the most dangerous hours of the day, and particularly during the early hours of the night. Very likely such a precaution may be most useful. The air enters the human frame through the mouth and the nose. In the latter it meets with a species of natural filter in the numerous windings of the nasal cavities; and the vibrating epithelium which lines those cavities, drives back towards the nostrils, the minute particles held in suspense by the inhaled air, and collected by the nasal filter. Any one can prove this to his own satisfaction, by remaining for a length of time in a room where smoking has been going on, before going to bed; when he blows his nose next morning, he will find his handkerchief stained with a slate-coloured mucus. That colour is produced by the minute particles of carbon in the smoke, which have entered the nose with the inhaled air, and which during the night have been driven back by the vibrating epithelium which lines the nasal cavities towards the opening of the nostrils. Those particles of carbon have a specific weight far greater than the specific weight of malaria germs; and therefore it is extremely probable that the nasal filter performs a useful function in malarious localities, by purifying the air which passes through the nose at every breath. But, in man, the greater portion of the air inhaled passes through the mouth into the lungs, and the cavity of the mouth has no filtering power, because it is wide, it has no inequalities, and is covered by a smooth epithelium. The adoption of an artificial filter at the opening of the mouth would assist the purifying of the inhaled air, which the nasal filter, in man, can only achieve in a very slight degree.

Another fact to be noted is, that in Rome, more than in any other place, it is necessary to guard against the effects of vases of flowers placed in living rooms. In 1879, during the course of our experiments respecting the malarious ferment, Klebs and myself were surprised at seeing how frequently soil gathered from malarious places, acquired a high degree of morbific power, when it was kept under the same condition as the earth in flower pots placed in a conservatory, or in sufficiently heated rooms. This seems to lead to the supposition, that the habit of keeping a quantity of live plants in very hot rooms, may prove dangerous when the earth in the pots has been taken from malarious places. And there is no doubt of the fact. It happens sometimes that in certain northern regions, perfectly free from malaria, cases of malarious infection have occurred, caused by no other reason than the accumulation in very hot rooms of flower vases, brought from foreign parts and containing malarious earth. Amongst the many examples which might be cited in support of that statement, one, and that a very convincing instance, will suffice. It was communicated to me by Eichwald, Professor of Medicine in the University of St. Petersburg.

Professor Eichwald had under his care in the north of Russia—at a place where no signs of malaria had ever been known—a lady affected by malaria fever, of a most obstinate character. The fever being very slight, was easily cured by means of small doses of quinine, and the cure lasted as long as the patient, after recovering, remained in her bedroom. It re-appeared, as soon as she resumed her daily habits. Those alternations of rapid cures and of equally prompt relapses, were repeated a good many times, until, a close investigation into the habits of the lady, revealed to Eichwald the cause of the disease. The lady used to spend the greater portion of the day, in a drawing-room, in which was a large collection of plants; and in that room, where the temperature was always very high, no sooner was she cured of an attack of fever, than she caught it again. Eichwald had all the plants removed, and from that day forth, the lady had no return of fever.

It is not difficult to realize, that in a country like Rome, the danger of introducing by such means, into the atmosphere of dwelling-houses, an amount of malarious germs, is greater than anywhere else, considering the spread of the malaria-ferment throughout that region, and the probability that the earth in flower-vases is more or less impregnated with it. It would be going too far to say, that no plants ought to be permitted in drawing-rooms, as that would be an exaggerated view of the case; but it is no doubt highly necessary, that great attention should be paid to the ventilation of the rooms in which they are kept, in order to guard against any possible accumulation of malaria-ferment in the air of such confined spaces. The danger is less when there is a fireplace in the room, for that acts as a ventilator; but it becomes more difficult to counteract when the room is warmed by heating-pipes.

In addition to the precautionary measures, tending to diminish the quantity of the malaria-ferment, which is absorbed into the system at every breath, popular experience has taught us others, the object of which is to prevent the germs, already absorbed, from remaining in the human body for any length of time. These all resolve themselves into expedients, for maintaining in an active and regular condition, the circulation of the blood. By means of an active and regular circulation, all the secretions of the body are kept in an active and regular condition; and, if the malaria-ferment be absorbed in moderate quantities, it is constantly being driven out. But, should the circulation be enfeebled, then the malaria-ferment has time to attack directly, the red globules of the blood (as Marchiafava and Celli have demonstrated), and thus to produce infection, which becomes either acute or chronic, according to the quantity of ferment absorbed, and according to the temperament of the individual. When the circulation becomes disturbed in any particular organ, the malaria-ferment remains confined within its blood-vessels. And, besides being thus placed in a most favourable condition for causing a general state of infection, it is enabled to produce specific inflammation in those organs where it chiefly resides.

In order to contend against those dangers, in all malarious countries it is sought to maintain the action of the circulating system by good nourishment, and by a moderate use of wines and spirits, and to avoid all disturbance of the system from variations of temperature. Even in those malarious regions, where the average temperature is high, and the summer heat is excessive, we find that the inhabitants are always warmly clad, for there is nothing they dread more than a chill, this being undoubtedly the most conducive cause to a development of fever. From that fact, many persons have concluded, that the malaria fever is not due to a specific ferment, but is simply the effect of a—so-called—rheumatizing action; that is to say, of a sudden lowering of the temperature to which the body has been exposed. This is a notion worthy of the days when pathology was in its infancy and upon the consideration of which we need not waste any time. Unfortunately, fevers often occur without any intervening rheumatizing causes, which in these, as in other diseases, only tend to give the morbific ferment already seated in the body a more rapid opportunity of developing its specific action. They disturb the circulation of the blood, checking its movement in some vessel-localities, and diminishing the activity of some of the secretions. In so doing, they retain in the blood the specific ferments which are there kept in suspense, and cause them to remain in the small vessels, where the movement of the blood has been slackened. In this way, they often help the development of cholera, of typhoid fever, of malarious infection, &c., in those persons into whose system the specific ferment of any one of those different diseases has already introduced itself. But they are powerless to produce such development in those persons whose bodies do not contain the specific ferment of any one of those diseases.

Experience has proved that it is necessary to continue the precautionary measures, tending to maintain the circulation of the blood in an active and regular condition, for some days after leaving a malarious region. It has happened, not infrequently, that persons who, by taking those precautionary measures, have been able to ward off attacks of malaria in Rome, even in the most unfavourable seasons, have had to succumb to them after leaving that city, because they have abandoned those measures at once. The elimination of the malaria-ferment from the body is a slow process, and any one who has been breathing poisoned air in malarious places, during any length of time, cannot, immediately on leaving the locality, do things which may disturb the circulation of the blood, without running the risk of bringing on an attack of fever. It is only after a certain length of stay in a wholesome atmosphere, that a new mode of life can be adopted, because then only, can the elimination of the malaria-ferment, be considered completely effected.

Thus it will be seen, that the precautionary measures suggested by popular experience, taken as a whole, are of considerable value. But it must be observed, that in order to carry them out properly, a person must enjoy a certain amount of independent means, and be able to lead a strictly regular life. To those who, in Rome, lead an exclusively city life, it is possible to adopt those measures for themselves and their families, even in the worst years. But those who have to lead an active life in the Campagna, and especially the unfortunate peasants, how is it to be expected that they can submit to those measures for at least three months in the year? And even were they able to do so, who can guarantee their immunity from attacks of malaria, when we know that, in the Agro Romano, malaria is so much more virulent than in Rome?

Mention has already been made of the experiment made at the Tre Fontane by convicts, and of the violent attacks of malaria which they often suffered. And in that instance, we had to deal with men submitted to an iron discipline, and on whom every sort of practical hygienic measure could be enforced, inasmuch as it was the Government that undertook the expense of lodging, feeding, and clothing them. Imagine, then, what would happen in a fixed settlement of free agriculturists, composed not only of adult males, who are much worse fed and clad than convicts, but also of women and children! The thought of what would happen in their case, and the earnest desire which, in common with so many others, I entertain of seeing the Agro Romano repopulated in the course of time, induced me to undertake the study of which I spoke towards the end of the preceding chapter: that is, to ascertain if it were not possible to render the human system less susceptible to the influence of malaria. The problem, in plain terms, may be thus stated;—inasmuch as we have not yet arrived at discovering the means of so improving land fit for cultivation, as to make it impossible for malaria to exist in it, is it possible so to modify the human organism as to render it proof against the poisonous effects of malaria-ferment?

The first idea which suggested itself, was a malarious vaccination, but unfortunately, that notion could not be entertained for a moment. Vaccination is of no practical use, except when infection is limited in its duration and so modifies the human body as to render it, for a greater or less period of time, proof against the attacks of the specific ferment which produces this infection. Such is the case with the infection of small-pox, which, as is generally known, begins and ends within a brief period of time, and leaves the human system in such a condition, as to enable it to withstand for a length of time, or for ever, all new attacks of the disease itself. That fact suggested to the medical men of the East, (the original habitat of small-pox), the idea of preserving people from the eventual attacks of a virulent small-pox, by inoculating them with the small-pox virus, taken from persons suffering from a mild attack of the disease, and thus subjecting them to an infection of a mild nature, in order to save them from the disease in a malignant form.

This system was introduced into Europe during the last century by Lady Mary Montagu, and subsequently improved upon by Jenner, who discovered that the same effect could be produced at a less risk, by inoculating with the virus taken from cows, instead of with human virus— hence the name of vaccine.

Pasteur, from this original fact, set himself the task of

discovering, if it were possible, to produce artificial vaccine, by which men and animals, might be preserved from other infections, similar in their course to that of small-pox. Once proved that an infection as powerful as that of small-pox, can have its virulence diminished by the simple fact, of its development taking place within one organic system instead of another, without, however, losing its power of rendering exempt from subsequent attacks of small-pox, those persons who have been inoculated with it, it was natural that the hope should be entertained of being able to modify in a similar manner the infectious power of other *morbigenous ferments*, by developing them through some particular mediums. In this way, Pasteur succeeded in reducing into true vaccine, the specific ferments of cholera in poultry, and of anthrax, and it is not improbable, that other similar artificial vaccines, may in the future be prepared, which will serve as a preventive against other infectious diseases, which do not repeat their attacks, except very rarely.

But malarious infection does not belong to that class of maladies. The duration of its course is indefinite, and cases have even been known, where a single attack has undermined the constitution, during a whole lifetime. Moreover, a first attack, instead of rendering a person less liable to subsequent returns, rather predisposes to future attacks. A person who has once suffered from malaria, although he may be completely cured of it, is more susceptible to its influence, than a person who has never had it. Hence it is that, even if it were possible to diminish artificially, the power of malaria-ferment, no one would dare to inoculate a healthy man with it, since by so doing, we should only render him more liable to attacks of the disease, from which he had previously been free.

For the same reason it is impossible to become acclimatized in a malarious country. If a person be possessed of an extraordinary amount of resisting power—that is to say, if he is able to offer a great amount of organic resistance to malaria, so as to repel its attacks on his constitution—he will escape it. But should he not be in that condition previous to venturing into a malarious country, he certainly will not obtain it there; his system will on the contrary deteriorate. His constitution, already insufficiently strong to resist the inroads of malaria, will become still less resistant after a first attack, even should he be perfectly cured of it. I do not pretend to be able to give a scientific explanation of the fact, for it would lead one into a maze of hypotheses, which have as yet, no secure foundation. But the fact is as I have stated, and the proof of it can be found in every malarious country.

Undoubtedly, the colonizing of malarious countries was above all things, the result of the acclimatization of the colonists; not indeed, of the *acclimatization of the individual*, which at all times has been an impossibility, but of a generic *acclimatization of the race*. Until the remedies, adapted to counteract the most virulent malarious infection, were discovered, the course of events was after this fashion: a band of colonists went into a malarious region, settled down there, and at once began to pay a heavy tribute in the loss of human life. This swept off, without any exception, all those who were unable to offer any specific resistance; it spared almost entirely, all such as were able to offer a stout resistance. The future prospects of the colony, depended upon the proportion which these latter bore to the weaker category. Should the proportion of the strong to the weak prove to be sufficiently great, the development of the colony was secured from the outset. This power of constitutional resistance, has been proved to be hereditary, and those repeated selections caused by malaria in each generation, conduced to the eventual increase of the resisting powers of the race, and that, to such a degree as to enable it to found powerful colonies in unhealthy sites, such as in Italy were those of Selinunte Agrigentum, Sibaris, Pœstum, and Rome.

The recollection of this natural selection, caused in ancient times by malaria, was preserved in the legend which existed, in several Greco-Italian cities, of a monster or demon, who being indignant at the invasion of the region belonging to him, devoured the inhabitants, but eventually was appeased, when the colony had afforded him a sufficient number of human sacrifices. There is a counterpart, in proof of this selection, as regards other endemic diseases, in times not far distant from the present. When Cortes invaded Mexico in 1519, he deemed it advisable to make a harbour on the shores of the Gulf of Mexico, at a spot where yellow fever raged with great virulence, and which developed eventually into the city of Vera Cruz, after yellow fever had caused an immense amount of mortality, amongst the colonists who had established themselves there. There is no known specific remedy against yellow fever, so that the natural selection caused by it, in the successive generations of the colony of Vera Cruz, has never been checked. At the present time, the settled population of Vera Cruz, is able to resist the attacks of yellow fever, to a degree which appears surprising, not only to strangers, but even to the Mexicans from the interior, who, whenever they have to visit that city on business, pay so large a tribute to the yellow fever, that they call it the City of the Dead (*Ciudad de los muertos*).

The immunity, also, which cattle and horses enjoy in malaria-stricken localities, may be considered as the result of a natural selection, caused by the malaria itself, during successive generations. The observations made by Grande, at Avole in Sicily, and by Doctor Vicchi, a distinguished veterinary surgeon of Rome, place the question beyond doubt. Foreign milch cows particularly, and especially those from Switzerland, suffer from attacks of malaria to a degree which interferes greatly with their breeding, and in many cases, English horses have been known to succumb to true pestilential malaria.

Analogous differences in the powers of resistance, are to be met with, in populations of the same race, according to the fact of their springing from places, which have been always healthy, or from districts, where in former times, malaria has exercised its power of natural selection. The latter are, even at the present day, much more capable than the former, of resisting the attacks of malaria, although the effects of the natural selection have been greatly reduced by the specific remedies, which have been so freely used during the last century, in all malarious districts throughout the world.

In fact, since the discovery of Peruvian bark, and still more since that of quinine, the human race has no longer been subjected, in malarious countries, to a selection tending to increase its powers of constitutional resistance, but rather, to an inevitable diminution of those powers. By the specific cures rendered so efficacious by means of such remedies, the lives of a great number of persons are saved, who possess but feeble powers of constitutional resistance to malaria, and who, in former times, would have undoubtedly succumbed to the attacks of malaria. And those persons, thus saved, propagate children who possess a still less power of resistance than their parents; inasmuch as the attack of malaria, to which these latter have been subjected, has already reduced the resisting power which they may be able to transmit to their children, and thus, from generation to generation, the human race reaches that point of physical degradation, which leaves such a painful impression upon those who visit districts badly stricken with malaria.

Consequently, we must abandon all hope of acclimatizing any portion of the civilized human race, by means of a process of natural selection. Our only hope, is to be enabled to produce an acclimatization by artificial expedients, which, to some degree at least, may prove a substitute for the action of the ancient process of selection, by increasing the constitutional powers of resistance, in those persons who have to live in malarious regions.

Various attempts have been made to obtain that object, by the daily use of quinine, of salicylates, or of the tincture of eucalyptus, but without any practical result. The salts of quinine are very expensive, and are not generally within reach of the means of the poorer peasantry—they produce an anti-malarious action which is rapid but fugitive, and after a long course, disturb the digestive organs and the nervous system. The salicylates when pure, cost a good deal, and, besides, it has not yet been proved, that they act as a preservative against malaria. The alcoholic tincture of eucalyptus may be beneficial (like most all other alcoholic drinks), by keeping the circulation of the blood in a state of activity, an essential thing in all malarious countries. Perhaps it may even act as preservative against light attacks of malaria. But, undoubtedly, it has not that effect, in regions where malaria is of a virulent character. This has been sufficiently proved, by the epidemics of fever from which the agricultural colony of the Tre Fontane has so often suffered, although it manufactures a tincture of eucalyptus of very good quality which, during the dangerous seasons, was served out to every member of that settlement.

In order to obtain a practical result, it is necessary to find a remedy, which shall exercise a lasting anti-malarious effect, which shall not be unpleasant to the taste, which shall not disturb any of the organic functions, and especially those of the digestion, and which, above all, shall cost little. The remedy that possesses all those qualities is arsenic. It had been observed in malarious countries, that many chronic attacks which defy the effects of quinine, often give way under the use of arsenic (arsenious acid): so much so, that ever since the invaluable discovery of quinine, arsenic has been freely used by medical men.

I had often had occasion to remark, that people who had employed the arsenical cure, in order to get rid of obstinate attacks of fever, with a successful result, were able to live in malarious countries without suffering a relapse. That fact induced me, in 1880, to try whether arsenic, administered daily in small doses, previous to the time of the fever season, and also during its duration, might not act as a preventive. Arsenic is not disagreeable to the taste, and may therefore be given to women and children without any difficulty; arsenic, moreover, does not disturb the digestive organs, when it is not introduced into an empty stomach, but rather aids digestion; and, besides, it costs little, and this is a point of great importance to poor people. I, consequently, decided to make the experiment, and as the first results which followed were most encouraging, I resolved, at the end of the year 1880, to continue the experiment on a wider basis during the subsequent years. I succeeded in inducing some large landowners of Tuscany and Rome, and the authorities of the Southern Railways, to try it on an extensive scale, in the year 1881. During that year also the results were encouraging; and in consequence, later on, some landowners of Puglia and of Sicily, and the authorities of the Roman Railways, determined to try the experiment upon the persons in their employ.

At the outset, an experiment of this kind is not easy to carry out. The very name of arsenic creates fear, not only amongst the common people, but even amongst medical men sometimes; and, consequently, the experiment fails, because it is not made boldly. But some intelligent men, and notably Dr. Ricchi, the Chief Medical Officer of the Southern Railways, succeeded in overcoming those difficulties, and placed the experiment upon a sure footing. The facts thus collected, seem to prove, that when arsenic is administered some weeks before the advent of the fever season, and is continued regularly during its duration, the human constitution is able to offer a better resistance to the attacks of malaria. Some individuals acquire a total immunity, others a partial one. The latter get fever sometimes; but their fever does not assume a malignant form and, even in districts where the malaria is of a dangerous character, they recover with the assistance of a little quinine. In the year 1883, for instance, Dr. Ricchi experimented upon seventy-eight persons in the district of Bovino, where malaria is very virulent. He divided them into two categories, one of which only, was subjected to the preventive system, by means of arsenic. At the termination of the fever season the following results were noted:—The great majority of those, who had not undergone the preventive system, had violent attacks of fever; and of those who had been subjected to the arsenical treatment, thirty-six escaped entirely, whilst the remaining three had slight attacks which they were able to shake off by the aid of quinine, and without having recourse to a doctor.

Amongst the experiments, successfully carried out during the summer of 1885, the very successful one tried upon the Revenue Guards in the district of Cervia (Province of Ravenna) by Dr. Magnani, was the subject of a Report which I made to the R. Accademia dei Lincei, at its sitting of December 6th, 1885 (Rendiconti, vol. i., p. 799). As a result of that communication, the Academy recommended the Minister of Finance to extend the experiment to all the Revenue Guards whose duties call them into malarious districts. Moreover, amongst the persons employed on the Southern Railways, although the development of malaria during the third quarter of 1885, was very considerable throughout all Italy, the results of the preventive system were satisfactory. Dr. Ricchi experimented upon 657 persons. In 402 cases the result was good, pretty good in 119, and indifferent in 136.

In the greater portion of these Italian experiments the patent arsenical gelatines of De Cian of Venice were used. These are soft tablets of gelatine, which contain a decigramme of arsenic, equally distributed through the tablet. Every tablet is divided into fifty squares, each of which contains two milligrammes of arsenic, and is wrapped up in paper; this renders the remedy easy to carry in the pocket or in a pocket-book, without the risk of its spoiling. In carrying out those extensive experiments, my coadjutors and myself, employed the patent gelatines, only because it was necessary that the doses of arsenic should be regularly administered. The liquid preparations of arsenic could not be adopted, as the use of them, except by exceedingly careful persons, is highly dangerous; because, in order that the preventive cure should be successful, it is necessary to commence (for adults) with a dose of two milligrammes a day, and gradually increase it to twelve milligrammes or more, daily. It is easy to understand how impossible it would be, to depend upon the exact doses being taken, if the liquid arsenic were used, in the case of an experiment being tried upon hundreds of individuals, many of whom, either from ignorance or carelessness, might do harm to themselves or to others, by an improper use of it. Amongst the solid preparations of arsenic, the patent gelatines are the safest. Each square (two milligrammes of arsenic) is easily torn off, like a postage stamp, and at a glance, when the administering is duly registered, it is easy to see that the proper doses have been taken. Besides, those gelatines are the only form of solid preparations of arsenic, which can be easily dissolved in coffee or in soup, (for arsenic is never to be taken on an empty stomach); whereas other solid preparations of arsenic often pass through the digestive tubes, without being dissolved, and consequently, without being absorbed into the system.

And that was proved during the experiments on the persons employed on the Roman Railways. These began in 1883 only, and were under the direction of a very able and conscientious man, Doctor Apolloni. He found great opposition on the part of his sanitary staff; but was able in 1883, by making use of the patent gelatines, to verify some benefit derived from the use of this preventive cure. In 1884, the General Health Department of the Roman Railways, ordered the employment of arsenical globules instead of the gelatines. From the first Dr. Apolloni was struck with the fact, that none of the patients put on any weight, (as should always happen during the course of an arsenic cure, provided the individual be not subjected to excessive exertions, beyond the amount which the nourishment he receives is able to sustain), and this led him to suspect that the arsenical globules were not absorbed. In fact, a series of very close observations, made in the Maremma and at the hospital of Pisa, proved that the greater part of the globules passed through the stomach and the intestines, without being dissolved. Consequently, the experiment tried by the Roman Railways in 1884 proved a failure.

It is advisable, therefore, whenever the experiment of the preventive cure by arsenic is to be made, through the administration of arsenic in a solid form, that the patent gelatines should be preferred. They are easy to take, assimilate quickly, and can be readily controlled.

Amongst the numerous experiments of this preventive cure, one of the most interesting is that made by Dr.

Leslie in the Congo Free State, where he acted as Government medical officer from 1885 to 1887. In tropical countries, such an experiment is very risky; because there, the malarious season lasts, more or less, throughout the whole of the year. Dr. Leslie succeeded in avoiding the dangers of such a protracted administration of arsenic, by interrupting it during fifteen days, every six weeks. He applied this cure on a large scale, from the Governor, Sir Francis de Winton, down to the poorest colonist. Dr. Leslie states that every one, who had gone regularly through the cure, was preserved from severe attacks of fever; that the most part of the persons under treatment, enjoyed complete immunity; and that those, who were attacked by malaria, got very slight fevers, which were easily cured with moderate doses of quinine. Those results, obtained in a tropical country, are highly encouraging to us, who have to deal with countries, where the malaria season is limited to a few months of the year.

Still, it must not be supposed, even were it definitively proved that arsenic increases, in a marked degree, the powers of resistance in the human system, against attacks of malaria, that there is nothing more to be done. No doubt it would be a great point gained; so great indeed, that, after many years of extensive and often, most successful experiments, I hesitate to declare it a success, because such important and vital considerations are involved, that a too hasty judgment ought not to be pronounced. But, supposing that this essential part of the question should be successfully solved, victory will not yet have been obtained.

The main object in view, it must be remembered, is to obtain, by means of those preventive measures, an increase in the average resistance of the human frame, against the attacks of malaria. In order, therefore, to obtain useful practical results, it is necessary that this average resistance should exist. If, from any cause whatever, it should be diminished, the experiment is liable to failure, and in fact does often fail. Of this we had a recent proof in the Agro Romano, at a station of Carabinieri, located in a region of virulent malaria, where every man had, by means of the arsenical preventive remedies, been able to keep free of fever through the malaria season, when, of a sudden, two of them were struck down by malaria fever, after having been enfeebled by acute secondary disease. Amongst the inhabitants of malarious districts, poverty, previous attacks of fever, and the weakness of the digestive organs, have already often reduced their powers of resistance to a minimum, when they have recourse to the preventive cure. Many cases of failure are due, as was first observed by Dr. Ricchi, to causes which it is not always possible to remedy. But still, something may be done in that direction, and Dr. Ricchi himself has already found a means of somewhat counteracting their effect. He sought to assist, those enfeebled frames in obtaining a normal average resistance, by administering a cheap, powerful, and easily digested aliment, in the shape of calves' blood. The blood is in the first place sterilized, then dried, and afterwards converted into a very fine powder. The name of " Trefusia " has been given to that preparation: it dissolves easily in every sort of liquid, and many clinical observations have proved, during the last few years, that it possesses re-constructive elements of great value.

It must be borne in mind, moreover, that the preservative which I have suggested, even should it be recognized as efficacious, could only be taken into general use with great difficulty. We have to contend with the fear, which the very name of arsenic produces; and great difficulties are constantly to be met with, in securing a due regularity in the administering of this remedy. Consequently, in all attempts which may be made, to colonize malarious districts, it will be necessary to employ some economical means, sure and innocuous, to combat chronic malarious infection. Persons, who are not intimately acquainted, with the miseries of malarious countries, only consider the dangers of acute fevers, which so often prove fatal. But those dangers, although great, are generally warded off, when medical aid is at hand. The real scourge of malarious countries is chronic malarious infection, which ruins families and deteriorates the race, undermining the vital powers, and producing a slow and progressive anæmia. This infection often resists every known remedy, and is even aggravated by a constant use of quinine, to which recourse is had, in order to check the attacks of fever which, from time to time, renew themselves. In fact, quinine becomes a poison of the vaso-motor nerves, after a prolonged use. Hence, it is absolutely necessary to find a more efficacious remedy, which shall be at the same time less injurious, and less expensive than quinine, to counteract those infections.

Amongst the popular remedies in use against attacks of malaria fever, those which have had the greatest repute, have ever been the preparations from the lemon-tree. Many of the inhabitants of Greece, of Arabia, and of Italy, make use of the juice of that fruit, either by itself, or in coffee; in many parts of Greece and of Italy, slight attacks of fever are treated with a decoction of the seeds of lemon; and in Guadaloupe, the inhabitants make use of the bark of the roots of the tree, dried and pulverized. The use of those traditional remedies renders it probable, that lemon-trees produce an anti-malarious substance, which seems to be more abundant in the fruit than in the other parts. In fact, the most active of all these popular remedies, is a decoction of the whole lemon fruit. Generally speaking, the preparation is thus made:—A lemon freshly gathered from the tree is taken, and cut into thin slices, then the slices, with the whole of their rind and seeds, are put to boil in three glassfuls of water, and kept in ebullition until reduced to one glassful. The liquid is then strained through a cloth, pressing out forcibly the remains of the boiled lemon, and then it is left to cool gradually. As a rule it is given to the patient in the morning.

That simple remedy, which costs so little, sometimes produces the most wonderful cures. The first time I heard of it, was from Dr. Maglieri, who had cured himself by it of a malaria fever, and I at once began to get it adopted in the Campagna of Rome. In some cases of obstinate fever, which neither quinine, nor even arsenic, could conquer, it produced such rapid and salutary effects that I considered myself justified in reporting upon it to the Minister of Agriculture, in a statement placed before him on March 18th, 1883. That induced several distinguished medical men, such as Dr. Mascagni of Arezzo, Dr. Ferraresi of Rome, and Dr. Cervello of Palermo, to try it in cases of chronic malarious infection which they were unable to overcome with the recognized specific remedies, and sometimes even in acute malaria cases. They succeeded in obtaining, in many instances, rapid and lasting cures, and besides, discovered that this simple remedy, stirred up the blood circulation of the abdomen, restored the appetite, and strengthened the digestive powers of the stomach: that is to say, it corrected some of the most serious functional derangements, to which the inhabitants of malarious countries are exposed. Later on, I learnt that an old doctor in my native mountains, in the upper valley of the Tiber, had enjoyed for many years, a reputation amongst the shepherds returning from the Maremma, of being able to cure cases of malaria, which appeared incurable, by a secret remedy of his own. Shortly before his death, he divulged the secret to a brother practitioner, Dr. Chini; it consisted of a decoction made in a similar manner to the one which I have already described, from the fruit of the lemon, or of the bitter orange. I laid all those facts before the International Medical Congress, held at Copenhagen on August 12th, 1884, and since then, the use of it has been adopted in Italy and elsewhere. Lately Dr. Shakspeare, of Philadelphia, informed me that he had tried the remedy in his hospital, in cases of most obstinate malarious infection, and that he sometimes obtained very satisfactory results.

I do not venture to say that it is a certain cure, because, before making such a statement, it must be subjected to a longer methodical trial than it has hitherto had. But, inasmuch as it is a most harmless remedy, and within the reach of all classes, I do not shrink from advocating it, nor from recommending all medical men, who practise in malarious districts, to make it as widely known as possible. Time will show if the hope of having discovered in it, a means of relieving the greatest scourge of malarious countries, is ill or well founded, but in the meanwhile, it ought to be tried. I have been told that it is an old woman's remedy, and it may be so; but that does not do away with its efficacy, and before rejecting it, we must give it a trial, and a very extensive trial.

In former chapters, I have had many occasions to show that, as far as malaria is concerned, a great deal more is to be learnt from the inhabitants of countries, which are afflicted by that plague, than from books. If that be true, as regards everything relating to the natural history of malaria, it is still more true respecting the treatment of the infection, which it engenders in the human organism. The great revolution effected in medicine by the discovery of the specific qualities of the Peruvian bark, (which subsequently led to the discovery of quinine, and enabled medical men to deal successfully with the worst forms of malaria fever), was not due to any scientific researches, and still less to the sagacity of the medical body. On the contrary, they opposed its adoption with the utmost tenacity, and it may be truly asserted, that the benefits which it has conferred upon the human race have been secured in the face of professional opposition. Its discovery is not even due to a civilized people, but to a semi-barbarous race. It so happened that at Lima, Countess Cinchon, wife of the Spanish Viceroy, who governed Peru in 1638, was taken ill of a most obstinate malarious fever. Whilst every one around her, abandoned all hope of her recovery, the chief judge of the province of Loja, arrived on the scene, and persuaded the Viceroy to induce her to take some powders, which were in common use amongst the natives of Peru, and which had cured him of a similar attack of fever. The Court doctors declared the thing impossible, and said that, supposing it had happened, it was due to witchcraft. It was only after the Superior of the Monastery of Loja had intervened, and asserted that some Peruvian pupils had taught his fellow-monks the use of those powders, that the Countess took them, and in the course of time was cured. That remedy was Peruvian bark, dried and pulverized. The Countess of Cinchon brought it to Europe, and it is in honour of her that the trees which produce that valuable remedy are now known as *cinchona* trees.

But it was a long time before the remedy was adopted by European doctors. Charles II. of England, who was fond of dabbling in natural science, had heard the new remedy spoken of, and when he caught a malaria fever in 1670, wished to try it. But Lower, his medical attendant, would not hear of it; and after the king was cured by secretly sending for a tincture of Peruvian bark prepared by Talbot (by means of which Louis XIV. of France also was subsequently cured), such ill-feeling was manifested against Talbot, by the London doctors, that the king was obliged to issue a proclamation, prohibiting the College of Physicians from persecuting Talbot.

And this was not the last of it. A hundred years after the introduction of this sovereign remedy into Europe, Frederick II. of Prussia, the great Frederick, was taken ill of a malaria fever in the year 1740. As the fever ran a protracted course, the king was anxious to try the effect of Peruvian bark, but his doctors did not believe in it, and managed to relieve him by the use of the ferruginous waters of Pyrmont, instead. It was only after being ill for two months, and when he had decided to invade Silesia, after the death of the Emperor Charles VI., that he ordered a supply of Peruvian bark, and got rid of his fever.

With such examples before us, it would be childish to abstain from making use of a remedy, recommended by popular experience, and already recognized as being efficacious in so many instances, simply out of consideration for the dignity of science. The vast majority of the remedies used in medicine, have found their way into the Pharmacopœia in a like manner; popular experience has discovered them, and doctors have only prescribed the mode of using them upon a rational system of doses. It is only of very late years that the progress of chemistry and of physiology has enabled us to take the first steps in instituting an experimental pharmacology—that is to say, a scientific "Materia Medica." If the use of Peruvian bark against attacks of malaria fever, had been postponed until such time as its most active principle—quinine—was discovered, and its physiological action methodically studied, malarious infections would have been treated until lately, in the same manner as during the Middle Ages. Since we already possess sufficient data to lead us to hope, that arsenic does act as a preservative, and that the decoction of lemon is a useful substitute for quinine, let us experiment upon the one and the other on every possible occasion. Should experience declare that the opinion is well founded, there is plenty of time to investigate later on, the scientific reasons of their beneficent action. In the meanwhile, numerous cases of individual suffering will have been relieved, and, perhaps, the work of founding colonies in malarious districts, may be undertaken with a greater chance of success.

Pardon & Sons, Printers, Wine Office Court, Fleet Street, E.C.

www.ingramcontent.com/pod-product-compliance
Lightning Source LLC
Chambersburg PA
CBHW031453160426
43195CB00010BB/959